Development

in

States of War

Selected articles from *Development in Practice*

Introduced by Stephen Commins

A Development in Practice Reader

Series Editor: Deborah Eade

Oxfam (UK and Ireland)

Available from the following agents:
for Canada and the USA: Humanities Press International, 165 First Avenue,
Atlantic Highlands, New Jersey NJ 07716-1289, USA; tel. (908) 872 1441; fax (908) 872 0717
for southern Africa: David Philip Publishers, PO Box 23408, Claremont, Cape Town 7735, South Africa; tel. (021) 644136; fax (021) 643358.

Available in Ireland from Oxfam in Ireland, 19 Clanwilliam Terrace, Dublin 2 (tel. 01 661 8544)

The views expressed in this book are those of the individual contributors, and not necessarily those of the editors, the publisher, or the editorial advisers.

Published by Oxfam (UK and Ireland), 274 Banbury Road, Oxford OX2 7DZ, UK
(registered as a charity, no. 202918)

Designed by Oxfam Design Department
Typeset in Gill and Baskerville
Printed by Oxfam Print Unit

Oxfam (UK and Ireland) is a member of Oxfam International.

Contents

Preface

Deborah Eade

It is now almost routine to begin an essay on conflict-related emergencies by stating that contemporary wars are fought not on demarcated battlefields, but in the towns, villages, and homes of ordinary people. The fact that 90 per cent of today's war casualties are civilians, and the fact that four out of five refugees and displaced persons are women and children (perhaps over 40 million people worldwide) are so often quoted that we hardly stop to think about what they mean. The end of the Cold War and the collapse of the Soviet bloc are thought to have intensified these trends and ushered in the New World Disorder and the concomitant phenomenon of the complex humanitarian emergency (CHE).[1] Humanitarian aid is no longer seen as being insulated from politics, nor are aid workers immune from attack when they assist civilians in war zones. Agencies, relief personnel, and humanitarian assistance are all subject to fierce and sometimes violent dispute. All, in various ways, can be manipulated to influence the outcome of conflict.

Experienced development and relief agencies know (but sometimes seem to have forgotten) that emergencies have always been complex. Twenty years ago, the 1976 earthquake that devastated Guatemala exposed that country's deep social, economic, and cultural rifts and sparked one of the most brutal, sustained, and comprehensive military campaigns against civilians in Latin America's violent history: a chain of events that led to its being dubbed an 'unnatural disaster'.[2] No international humanitarian aid programme since World War II — whether Europe in 1945–6, Palestine in 1948, Biafra in 1968–70, Ethiopia in 1974 and 1986, or Cambodia in 1979 — could usefully be described as simple, in either political or operational terms. So it may seem almost perverse to define certain emergencies as 'complex', as though others were somehow not.

However, the term 'complex emergency' was coined in the United Nations to describe those major crises, which have indeed proliferated since 1989, that require a 'system-wide response': a combination of military intervention, peace-keeping efforts, relief programmes, high-level diplomacy, and so on.[3] In other words, the complexity refers to the 'multi-mandate' nature of the international response as well as to the multi-causal nature of the emergency; to the recognition that major crises are necessarily political and economic (in their causes as well as their consequences), and never 'merely' humanitarian; and to our engagement as humanitarian agencies in this reality as much as it refers to the reality itself.

The world may or may not be a more complex place than it used to be — though we should beware of inventing a mythical Golden Age of shared moral certitudes, 'clean' wars, and the uncontested simplicities of administering first aid to war casualties. But our *understanding* of how humanitarian relief fits into the international scene has undeniably had to become more intelligent, and more critical, in recent years. We have had to learn to see beneath the surface, to hear what is not spoken, in framing humanitarian interventions. Gender analysis offers a useful analogy. Only a decade or so ago, relief workers could content themselves with consulting with the village headmen or 'community leaders' about what was going on, and what they thought was needed; and then draw up a response on that basis. In those days, any such consultation with the 'victims' was seen as an enlightened advance on earlier practice. Yet societies are not a linear hierarchy, in which those at the top represent the interests of everyone, including those at the bottom of the pile. They are a tangled web of relationships based on exclusion as well as inclusion, and permeated by diverse perspectives and life experiences. With this insight, deciding how to act for the benefit of women and children, as well as of men, becomes a more demanding (and certainly more time-consuming) matter. This is not because gender roles and identities have become more complex. Rather, it is because we have (or should have!) a deeper appreciation of how they shape people's needs; and have learned that ignoring such gender dynamics is most damaging precisely to those who most need support. Similarly, the politico-military dimension of emergencies is not new; but understanding how it influences relief programmes does indeed challenge many deeply held beliefs about neutrality and justice.

A regrettable consequence of viewing the end of the Cold War as the global watershed for humanitarianism is a tendency to dismiss earlier experience as having nothing to offer us today. As Stephen Commins stresses in his introductory essay, nothing could be less true. If we turn our backs on the past, we not only lose the opportunity to learn from experience, but may also misread the present. Written by practitioners from many different backgrounds and countries, this compilation of papers from *Development in Practice* shows that, to be effective, interventions must always be based on the recognition that societies in crisis retain and are shaped by their own past — one that pre-dates the arrival of the international aid juggernaut, CNN television, or the Blue Berets.

Survival may appear to depend on international assistance, but the future must be built by the actual survivors, long after the dust has settled.[4]

Its all-encompassing nature can make the impact of modern warfare both randomly impersonal and yet highly intimate. Political disappearances, 'ethnic cleansing', and gross violations of human rights — whether in Guatemala, Burma, Indonesia, Rwanda, or ex-Yugoslavia — are designed to destroy a society through systematic terror and hatred; and to destroy individuals through fear, pain, and loss. The millions of anti-personnel mines strewn across the paddy-fields of Cambodia or the small-holdings of Angola ensure that this cruelly indiscriminate destruction will continue for generations to come. Mending lives and relationships will demand patience, trust, and immense courage. For a society that has been ripped apart by civil war, developing a shared and sustainable vision of justice and peace may prove yet more complex than the emergency itself.

Deborah Eade
Editor, *Development in Practice*

Notes

1 The terms 'complex emergencies', 'political emergencies', 'complex political emergencies' (CPEs), and 'complex humanitarian emergencies' (CHEs) are used interchangeably. Here, following the practice of many humanitarian agencies, we use the latter.

2 See, for example, Roger Plant (1978): *Guatemala: Unnatural Disaster*, London: Latin America Bureau.

3 A document produced by the UN Department of Humanitarian Affairs, *Protection of Humanitarian Mandates in Conflict Situations*, states that '... given the inter-related causes and consequences of complex emergencies, humanitarian action cannot be fully effective unless it is related to a comprehensive strategy for peace and

security, human rights and social and economic development'.

4 The annotated bibliography in this volume cites several works addressing the consequences for civilians of the twelve-year war in El Salvador, which might serve as a microcosm of the complex emergency. These works portray both the broad and the specific policy dilemmas and practical issues implicit in providing humanitarian assistance to civilians, refugees, displaced people, and returnees in a climate of counter-insurgency and hostility to such intervention. They also show the complexities of embarking on post-war reconstruction in a post-Cold War environment of economic liberalisation. See Larkin *et al.* (1991); Macdonald and Gatehouse (1995); Pearce (1986); Thompson (1996; 1997 *forthcoming*).

In the line of fire:
development in conflict

Stephen Commins

The blurred continuum

International non-governmental organisations (NGOs) and other humanitarian agencies have traditionally assumed a dichotomy between relief and development work. Sometimes, this dichotomy has been reinforced by the way in which bilateral donor bureaucracies allocate funds for programmes and projects. Occasionally, as **Jonathan Goodhand** and **Peter Chamberlain** illustrate in their paper on NGOs in Afghanistan, reprinted in this volume, donors have even refused to support projects in what are deemed as relief areas if the programmes are 'too developmental'. Over the past decade, there has been a move towards establishing clear links, both conceptual and operational, between initial relief operations and longer-term development goals. Indeed, there is now a common language to describe 'the continuum' between relief and development work. This has proved helpful in contexts of food-insecurity and drought, but changes in the nature of emergencies demanding a humanitarian response now require the recognition that both the old dichotomy and the new continuum may obscure more than they clarify. The difference between relief and development has been substantially blurred in situations of long-term political emergencies related to civil conflict. What is now apparent is that some forms of gap-filling development work to provide stabilising mechanisms can be done, and are indeed necessary, in situations of conflict.

A changed environment: new skills and challenges

Operations in conflict-related emergencies require different skills and time-frames, and a recognition that local communities have their own resources and priorities, and are not helpless victims, even in situations of brutality and suffering. The experiences of NGOs operating in such situations can provide a valuable base for helping other agencies to identify development potential within conflict, to review their priorities and capacity for work in different settings, and to present policy challenges to governments and donors. Without an understanding of the ways in which development can and does occur on the midst of conflicts, NGOs will miss opportunities to strengthen local communities. Further, without a political and/or a human-rights perspective on conflicts, NGOs may either unintentionally strengthen warring groups, or serve as political cover for the lack of action by donor governments.

NGOs have begun to move, however uncertainly, towards a wider understanding of development, which is not limited to economic indicators. They have come to recognise that there are questions of social relations, production relations, gender, and the management of human capacity and natural resources that need to be considered. In order to achieve lasting and real changes, they need to understand development as a more inclusive concept that cannot be contained in the old linear continuum of 'relief-to-rehabilitation-to-development'. The new concepts do not view development as depending on the end of armed hostilities, because they include relations and capacities that require attention even during conflicts — as can be seen from the experiences of agencies in places as diverse as Sudan and El Salvador.

Reflections for fresh insights

This Reader is a collection of papers from previous issues of *Development in Practice*, offering a range of perspectives on the challenges that confront NGOs in situations of conflict. The designation 'NGO' is often over-inclusive (one colleague described 'NGO' as equivalent to calling a table 'not water'); but, for the purposes of this essay, it includes local, national, and international NGOs, with an emphasis on the roles of the latter in the context of conflict. The relationship between international NGOs and local organisations is often complex, as is clear from several of the papers in this Reader. Learning from these experiences is not a matter of finding answers to simple or linear questions; rather the papers can help practitioners to recognise their own perspectives and assumptions about working in conflict, the importance of providing policy input to governments and humanitarian agencies, the need to review the priorities of their own organisations, and questions related to operational practice.

If the experiences from the mid-1970s onwards are inadequately understood, NGOs will miss opportunities to improve their effectiveness while operating in the line of fire; their goals may be at odds with community perceptions; and, as observers such as Mary B. Anderson and John Prendergast have pointed out, they may worsen rather than alleviate the conflict.[1] The provision of food and other resources, the hiring of armed guards, agreements with particular political factions, or the selection of specific regions in which to concentrate can all have an influence on contending factions and even on the eventual outcome of the conflict. In a world where situations of long-term conflict are on the increase, these papers offer insights that will be a valuable resource for practitioners.

Complex humanitarian emergencies and 'the new reality'

The end of the Cold War in 1989 has been seen as creating the conditions for increased civil strife and internal wars.[2] There is a danger in implying that 1989 was the date on which complex humanitarian emergencies (CHEs) came into being. Instead, it may be that the removal of super-power restraints on client states has also been accompanied by growing awareness of the spread of such emergencies. These are characterised by the breakdown of political, economic, and social orders, and by the targeting of civilian populations for violence. The cruel realities of today's CHEs can be found in the earlier civil wars in which NGOs gained important experience in the 1970s and 1980s. For example, there were many significant and brutal emergencies before 1989 (in places such as Afghanistan, Mozambique, Cambodia, and El Salvador), but these were overshadowed by the Cold War, and many were somewhat muted by the actions of various external actors. They share with more recent crises the character of being political, rather than natural, emergencies. And as such they are important sources of information and experience that can provide guidance for practitioners today.

The Cold War was a time of vicious, proxy wars. While the patrons have been removed, the arms and sources of conflict have not. The growth of CHEs is documented in the increased numbers of refugees since 1990, the growing numbers of internally displaced persons (IDPs), and the higher proportion of official development assistance (ODA) now spent on emergency relief. One result of the recognition of the realities of working in long-term CHEs is a rethinking of the role of NGOs in these conflicts. The harsh lessons from experiences such as Rwanda, Somalia, and Bosnia point to the need for NGOs to give serious attention to how they operate in such contexts. Increased recognition of the difficulties of working in situations of armed conflict should not detract from lessons that have been learned in the past two decades. Because of the decline of security issues related to the Cold War, greater attention has been paid to other kinds of conflict. In particular, the unravelling of a number of states in Africa has created the impression for some that the work of NGOs in situations of conflict is fairly new. However, this is far from the case, as can be seen when reviewing the range of NGO experiences in several long-term conflicts around the world before 1989.

Although there has been a tragic increase in the overall number of CHEs involving warfare and violence, over the past several decades many NGOs have gained significant experience of working in the line of fire. As the papers on Sudan and El Salvador in this volume point out, NGOs (local and international) which have worked with local communities in times of conflict have learned valuable lessons. Other places in which long-term development work has been done in the context of conflict include Ethiopia, Mozambique, Afghanistan, and Cambodia. In this Reader, the paper by **Alison Joyner** on work in Sudan provides insights into the task of incorporating development goals into long-term work with refugee populations. As she notes, it is 'too late to wait until after the emergency'. In this case, the introduction of a flexible system for educating teachers offers an approach for human development that is not contingent upon investing in buildings that might not survive the war. Joyner notes that, even in prolonged conflicts, depending on the nature of the warfare, societies will continue to 'develop' through crisis periods. If NGOs can also be flexible and mobile in their efforts, then improved education and training becomes an investment in people which can survive physical destruction. This is echoed by **Francisco Alvarez Solís** and **Pauline Martin**, writing about El Salvador, who conclude that 'a wealth of experience has been accumulated in humanitarian assistance, non-formal education and community-based health, economic and social development, particularly in areas and communities most severely affected by war'. The very difficulties inherent in assessing the impact of assistance in unstable environments point to the importance of enhancing local capacities in this area.

Building on local institutional capacities and local learning

As noted earlier, the relationship between international NGOs and local organisations is complex in ways that require attention and astute responses. NGOs experience tensions over the use of funds and programme priorities, as well as the problem of sub-contracting. International NGOs, in particular in emergency-relief situations, often operate as implicit or explicit sub-contractors for multilateral and bilateral donors. When they begin to work with local NGOs or grassroots organisations, there is a danger that, due to pressures of time and the larger operational structure within which they must function, the relationship will be established on a contractual basis for reasons of expediency. A further risk is that the pressure to 'go operational' will reduce the ability of international NGOs to assess their potential counterparts. Yet the task of assessing the legitimacy and accountability of different local organisations raises important issues that require careful analysis.

In civil conflicts, there are often new roles for local NGOs and grassroots organisations that stretch them in their operations and skills. Local organisations such as labour unions, churches, peasant cooperatives, and women's groups may move into different aspects of relief and rehabilitation work, out of necessity. This transition can cause difficulties when conflicts die down or cease, as Goodhand and Chamberlain, as well as Alvarez Solís and Martin, point out. New roles, new tasks, and even new structures emerge from conflict and must then adapt when conflict diminishes. In the Salvadorean civil war, many local groups emerged to defend community resources and provide for survival; and it was indeed in response to violence that new forms of social organisation evolved. This is also a reminder to international NGOs that they should be seeking locally generated forms of organisation to act as their partners and as the lead agencies in the community, rather than seeking to generate their own structures or projects. Assessing the realities in Central America, Alvarez Solís and Martin point out that 'many of the 1980s generation of NGOs are essentially the institutional expression of sectors of the urban and rural poor who organised to defend themselves from violence and oppression'. Given the enormous differences in country or regional contexts, the capacity or legitimacy of local NGOs cannot be taken for granted and requires astute on-the-ground assessment by those agencies which would support them.

Work in El Salvador, Cambodia, Sudan, and other countries has provided NGOs with lessons about, among other things, how development for survival occurs in the midst of conflict. The line between 'relief' and 'development' disappears, especially when one recognises that local populations have lives and histories that pre-date the presence of external agencies (as James Scott and Robert Chambers have emphasised). The challenge for NGOs is to understand the geographic spread and impact of contemporary conflicts, as well as the long historical time-frame. This comes though clearly in Goodhand and Chamberlain's paper on Afghanistan, where NGOs are forced to recognise that their work is occurring in situations of complexity and multi-layered realities. Similarly, the paper by **Chris Roche** offers insights into operating in turbulence and shows the possibility of finding stabilising points which do not resolve the conflict, yet may provide a foundation or base for future development.

As NGOs learn from their experiences in CHEs, they have to confront questions about their wider roles and responsibilities, especially in relation to the victims of violence. There has been an accepted distance between NGOs and other humanitarian agencies in relation to the politics of warfare and civil conflicts. This has begun to change, as NGOs' conduct in complex emergencies comes under closer scrutiny. The increased presence of NGOs in contexts of long-term conflict has created greater questions about the impact and role of any humanitarian agencies in such situations. Serious questions about their impact have been raised by commentators who have challenged NGOs to consider the real nature of their roles in multi-mandate operations. (The annotated bibliography in this volume contains examples.)

Lost neutrality and other complications

Mary B. Anderson has shown that there are many ways in which NGOs can exacerbate conflict. Frequently, the introduction of external resources has been interpreted as either favouring one side against another, or providing invaluable material that enhances the power of factional leaders. When NGOs hire guards or negotiate agreements with particular leaders, they move from a neutral role to one which may influence the outcome of the conflict. Anderson's concerns are echoed here by Alvarez Solís and Martin, who comment that the contribution of NGOs in El Salvador was not entirely positive, as they also brought competition, duplication, poor planning, lack of coordination, and generally weak evaluation of their work. They also point to the difficulties that arise from competition between NGOs for funding, and the tensions between NGOs and popular organisations. A problem which afflicts many NGOs, and not only in situations of conflict, is the increasing reliance on packaging and selling projects to donors.

These types of criticism are welcome and necessary, because during the 1980s there was a tendency to generalise about the attributes of NGOs, without a concomitant willingness to ask hard questions about the quality of their work. NGOs are under growing scrutiny regarding their legitimacy, accountability, and effectiveness.[3] There is a need to evaluate their impact and determine how accountability to local populations can be balanced with the requirements of different donors to NGO programmes. And accountability is also required when NGOs respond to hard political questions arising from conflict.

The organisation African Rights has produced trenchant criticisms of the shortcomings of international agencies in Somalia, Sudan, and Rwanda. Its Discussion Paper *Humanitarianism Unbound?* questions the role of humanitarian agencies and asks whether there is a new imperialism and arrogance among those who call for military action or 'humanitarian intervention' as a quick fix to complex emergencies.[4] A question that emerges from this critique and from the wider literature is whether humanitarianism is un-bound or has unravelled. Have NGOs called for intervention through arrogance, or rather as a result of their uncertainty about what to do in situations of conflict?

Security risks, violence, and psychosocial trauma

If NGOs accept that they are working in the context of emergencies that are political, and that often involve widespread and deliberate violence against civilians, they should not keep silent. But how they should convey their concerns about human rights and political issues is not always clear. **Alex de Waal**, the co-author of many African Rights reports, notes in this volume that the point of entry for human-rights concerns during famines may be the issue of the denial of food to civilians, for political rights are crucial to fighting famine.[5] **Miloon Kothari** makes similar points in the observation that forced evictions and uprooting of people and communities are becoming a recurrent aspect of conflict and government power-plays. The brutalisation of civilians, by famine or forced displacement, demands a clear role for NGO advocacy at a policy level, as well as provision of immediate relief.

Even as NGOs struggle to find ways to address dilemmas concerning human rights and political questions within conflicts, they are also faced with the emotional toll of violence on both their own workers and on civilian populations. A seminal essay[6] by Hugo Slim on 'endangered chameleons' underlines the increased targeting of humanitarian workers, who had previously been able to operate in a neutral space between combatants. NGOs have had a sense of protection and uniqueness which has encouraged them to operate in such situations, in the belief that risks were fairly low. This has changed with the increase in kidnapping and armed theft and even intentional targeting of NGO staff for violence. Slim's identification of the security issue and the psychological toll on NGO staff has been borne out in Rwanda, Burundi, and Liberia, as elsewhere, where NGOs and other humanitarian agencies have had offices attacked, staff killed and wounded, and threats delivered to their personnel by various military factions.

The demand on NGOs to operate in situations of conflict and high risk is paralleled by the challenges of working with traumatised populations. The papers in this volume by **Hàns Buwalda, Lucy Bonnerjea**, and **Jane Shackman** and **Jill Reynolds** all point to the costs imposed on civilians that often last longer than the need for food, shelter, or health-care services. These three papers all address social costs borne by communities caught up in warfare. At the same time, as **Derek Summerfield** stresses, it is important to note that these communities and their residents are not passive victims, nor are they simply 'trauma cases'. Again, there are complex historic and political circumstances in each situation, to which NGOs must be sensitive when planning and conducting their operations.

Developing wider experimental resources

The papers in this Reader provide several paths for NGOs working during conflicts or after their formal cessation. There cannot be one answer to the question of how NGOs should operate within such settings. But to encourage thinking within NGOs and by practitioners, these papers have been chosen to bring together the diverse experiences of NGOs and practitioners, and so to offer starting points for reflective questions and for generating new ideas out of organisational learning.

There are indications that NGOs and other humanitarian agencies are giving greater attention to the dilemmas presented by working in complex emergencies. Along with the just criticism that NGOs compete at times for resources and media coverage, the level of cooperation among NGOs, both at the national and international levels, has increased substantially in the past five years. Evidence for this is seen in the efforts of umbrella bodies such as the International Council of Voluntary Agencies (ICVA) and the NGO coordination with United Nations Department of Humanitarian Affairs (DHA). This is happening both in terms of operational work and in the interests of establishing a stronger and more coherent policy voice. There is interest in establishing mechanisms for giving accreditation to individual NGOs for different sectoral skills, partly to modify the media-driven and resource-driven nature of NGO work. Further, important questions are being asked about the difference between neutrality and independence in situations of egregious human-rights violations.

In conclusion, there are several wider issues that require further elaboration. The following questions may serve as the basis for greater reflection within and between agencies.

• Given the widespread violations of human rights that are committed in some political emergencies, do NGOs believe in the use of lethal force?

• In view of the longer-term nature of political emergencies, what are the best policy roles for different NGOs, especially in relation to the root causes of such conflicts?

• How can NGOs extend their time-frame for working in conflict situations?

• What are the challenges to the bureaucratic and administrative management of relief and development programmes in the context of complex emergencies?

• Can NGOs ignore the urge to ensure their own institutional survival and work for coherence and common programme standards?

• Are NGOs willing to address staff-capacity issues, as well as the question of credentials or codes of conduct for working in complex emergencies?

• How can NGOs respond to the challenges of new staffing and personnel roles, as well as new types of teams?

• Are there operational roles for NGOs in situations where they have no previous experience?

• How can NGOs most effectively 'scale up' from field experience to policy-making and become public voices for the victims of violence?

• How can NGOs 'scale down' or redirect their work to be attuned to the communities' own perceptions of their survival and development needs?

These questions are meant to encourage all NGOs and individual practitioners to think creatively about alternative futures. NGOs could become little more than ladles in the global soup kitchen, superficially alleviating the misery of the victims of conflict, but lacking the capacity, understanding, or interest to address its causes and consequences. NGOs may also become public-sector contractors for large donors; but, if so, can they retain independent voices and engage in well-informed actions in difficult situations?

Experience of working in situations of armed conflict has shown that opportunities for adaptive and creative programmes do exist, even when to the outsider it appears that little or nothing can be accomplished. The paper by

Chris Roche offers both a challenge and an opportunity for NGOs to establish stabilising points for their operations. Despite both international and national dislocations, NGOs can build accepted frameworks for working and interpreting what is happening. Even in the face of rapid, discontinuous, or turbulent change, where old assumptions are no longer valid, it may indeed be possible for NGOs to operate in the line of fire with effectiveness, accountability, and positive long-term impact.

The author

Stephen Commins has an extensive background in policy advice for a range of non-governmental and other organisations in the United States, and has for the last six years been working for World Vision International. He was previously Director of the Development Institute, Center for African Studies, at the University of California in Los Angeles, and he has written and published widely on development and food-security issues.

Notes

1 Mary B Anderson: 'Relationships between Humanitarian Agencies and Conflict and Remedial Steps that Might be Taken', unpublished paper presented at the Symposium on Humanitarian Assistance and Conflict in Africa, 1995; also, *International Assistance and Conflict: an Exploration of Negative Images*, (1994), Issues Series No. 1, The Local Capacities Peace Project, Collaborative for Development Action.

2 Mark Duffield: 'Complex Emergencies and the Crisis of Developmentalism' (see Annotated Bibliography).

3 Michael Edwards and David Hulme (1996): *Non-governmental Organisations: Performance and Accountability — Beyond the Magic Bullet*, London: Earthscan/SCF.

3 African Rights (1994): *Humanitarianism Unbound? Current Dilemmas Facing Multi-Mandate Relief Operations in Political Emergencies*, Discussion Paper No 5, London.

5 See also Jean Drèze and Amartya Sen (1989): *Hunger and Public Action*, Oxford: Clarendon Press.

6 Hugo Slim: 'The Continuing Metamorphosis of the Humanitarian Professional: Some New Colours for an Endangered Chameleon' (see Annotated Bibliography).

Operationality in turbulence:
the need for change

Chris Roche

Introduction

The Agency for Cooperation and Research in Development, ACORD,[1] is an operational NGO which, under certain conditions, undertakes so-called relief and rehabilitation activities within Africa. Its first priority is to facilitate the emergence of local organisations and structures, to enhance the socio-economic position of poor people in Africa. It defines *operationality* as *continuous presence*, and works where this is required, over a limited period, with the people it supports.

In Africa, it is now estimated that some 40 million people are in need of emergency assistance as a result of war, famine, insecurity and, increasingly, the effects of AIDS. In the past, crises or disasters[2] such as war and famine were seen by ACORD as temporary blips which were 'unusual'; it was assumed that 'normal' conditions would resume after a time. Inherent in the organisation's thinking was some idea of a continuum of relief—rehabilitation—development; while crises were viewed as setbacks on a path that had to be weathered before continuing the journey. There has, however, been a gradual realisation that such assumptions are no longer valid.

What are the implications for NGOs? How do we respond to the depth and rapidity of change in the world around us? What does development mean in such circumstances? How do we balance short- and long-term needs, the distribution of relief and provision of services with the nurturing of sustainable self-reliance, and the implementation of operational activities with concerns about human rights and political freedoms?

The need for new ideas

Unpredictability and crisis are a fact of life, even in the West, where it is becoming clear that 'sustainable growth' is over. In the African context, some have argued that the very survival of the continent is at stake. Such failures require us to rethink what we do in the face of this crisis for development thinking and practice (Hettne 1990). Can NGOs continue to respond to unexpected fluctuations and oscillations in their traditional way — that is, by ignoring them, or reacting after the event?

There are new ways of thinking about, and managing, change — for example in the areas of catastrophe,[3] chaos,[4] and complexity[5] theories. In fact, nothing less than a paradigm shift has been suggested.[6] For, if development is about the process of change, we need a more refined analysis of what change is.

On change[7]

For many years, natural and social sciences tended to concentrate on those aspects of change that are **smooth, linear, ordered, and predictable** — in other words, those types of change that are easiest to analyse, or those that some have described as leading to 'tame' problems. But **rapid, discontinuous, turbulent change**, such as occurs when a *coup d'état* happens or a currency is suddenly devalued, has tended to be ignored, basically because it is more difficult to measure, predict, and handle. However, most development problems are 'wicked', not 'tame', and involve just such types of discontinuous change. An analysis of 'wicked' (or turbulent) change can illuminate how we can support people to cope with and promote change, as well as how we might organise ourselves to do so.

• **Interdependence:** Real problems are caused not by one factor, but by many interdependent factors. For instance, a famine can be caused by drought, rising cereal prices, declining animal prices, poor roads, and lack of food aid — all at the same time. It is not one factor that is the cause, but the *combination* of them which leads to famine.

• **The butterfly effect:**[8] Small changes can produce large, and very divergent, effects under the right conditions. This indicates how important it is to try to understand what happened at the outset of turbulence. For example, in Niger in 1990, the fact that aid agencies did not provide food aid to nomads recently returned from Algeria led to demonstrations that eventually resulted in the rebellion in Mali. This small incident did not *cause* the rebellion, but was one of the sparks that *provoked* it. In essence, it set off changes that were already embedded in the processes of latent revolt in the area.

• **Feedback:**[9] Feedback enables organisms to adapt and develop and ultimately survive changing circumstances. It is also the mechanism by which variables inter-relate with and alter each other. The result of one process is the input for another. Feedback is essential, if we are to adapt to circumstances that vary rapidly and unpredictably. For NGOs, this means that the ability to monitor our work and alter things accordingly is the key to coping with change.

• **Patterns of change:**[10] The map-makers of the Middle Ages made great voyages possible, because they boldly put forward their ideas

without having seen the continents they drew. The shape was more important than the detail. If the exact details cannot be known, what can be said about the overall shape? In northern Mali in 1991, the ACORD team, after analysing the situation, looked at several different scenarios, ranging from the optimistic to the pessimistic, and then developed *'la méthode inversée'* (basically a process which involved partners visiting ACORD or sending messages rather than ACORD visiting them), a way of working which would have been possible under all but the most dangerous situations.

• **Stabilising points:**[11] Although situations never repeat themselves exactly, they often focus around certain stable points. It is important to understand what these stable points might be. In Somalia, for example, in many areas it is the elders who have proved to be the most stable element in the current crisis, and agencies have been able to build upon their influence and knowledge to distribute relief goods and initiate rehabilitation activities.

Food crises and conflicts are not exceptional or static events, but are rooted in the past. As expressions of struggles over power and rights, they are but a moment in existing processes of political, social, and economic change, the effects of which vary by class and gender. Strategic intervention demands an understanding of these processes of change. This means understanding that each crisis is different; and, as Michael Watts (1991) suggests, each is the product of interlinked and mutually determined factors, including:

• long-term processes, producing patterns of vulnerability, such as soil erosion or declining terms of trade;
• contingent or proximate events, producing reductions in resources and/or entitlements, such as war or drought;
• the specificity of local factors, such as social structures and access to and control over resources, which gives a particular 'rhythm and timbre' to vulnerability (for instance culture, or gender relations).

The need for a mix of responses

So what has all this got to do with development *in practice*? In contemporary Africa, we could classify degrees of turbulence as follows:

1 situations where *the community is engulfed in severe crisis*;
2 situations where *crisis is threatening*;
3 situations where *the community is recovering or rebuilding*;
4 situations where the *community is dealing with long-term trends*, or smooth change, and agencies can support people's ability to cope with and promote change: situations where some might say that 'sustainable development'[12] was possible.

ACORD's assistance has tended to fall into three types: material input through grant, sale, or credit; technical input, such as technical assistance or training; and organisational and moral support. What is striking about ACORD's experience is how far it has been possible to provide all of these in nearly all circumstances, except where life is physically threatened. Capacity-building can and should be as much a need in the face of severe crisis as in a more settled situation. Similarly, the strengthening of local coping mechanisms and political protection and lobbying are needed just as much by communities dealing with long-term trends as by those dealing with crisis.

ACORD's experience also illustrates that change can have a vastly different impact on different members of a community. It is thus essential to determine the distinct needs of men and women, and of people with different livelihoods, in the face of crisis. The role and functions of ACORD are determined by *whom* it is aiming to support, as much as by the overall situation. Examples from recent experience which lead to this analysis include the case of Somalia, where staff recognised the need to support poor female entrepreneurs involved in food preparation who were being put out of business by food distributions: ACORD's response was to give loans to enterprises in Port Sudan to allow them to manufacture pallets for agencies moving food-aid through the port, and to make tents for refugee populations.

When the margin between 'falling over the edge' and being able to survive without the charity of others is so small, aid agencies must concentrate on enabling people to avoid being caught in a downward spiral by finding new economic niches and using the market,[13] as well as providing for more immediate needs.

Figure 1 (overleaf) illustrates the pattern by demonstrating that, although it is likely that the major thrust of support in a situation of severe crisis will be towards meeting immediate needs, there are also needs which relate to capacity-building, income-generation, and institutional development.

This analysis suggests that the conventional division of programmes into the categories of relief, rehabilitation, or development is not only unhelpful but — more importantly — does not reflect local reality, where roles normally associated with 'development' are possible in 'relief' situations, and *vice versa*. For example, social security payments in industrialised countries, or guaranteed employment schemes or other safety nets for the most vulnerable in developing nations, could be described as 'relief', although many would see them as an essential facet of 'developed' societies. As Drèze and Sen (1989) have illustrated, in their detailed studies of countries which dealt with famines, governments which *integrated* relief, rehabilitation and development rather than *dividing* them into components of an evolutionary process are those which have had the most success in alleviating hunger. What is needed, therefore, is an adequate mix of responses.

Famine and war are about struggles for food and, ultimately, power. If emergency or humanitarian assistance is strictly defined in terms of food aid and medical relief, it runs the risk of weakening and undermining local production systems, local organisations, and local self-esteem. This in turn may lead to a weaker civil society and the reinforcement of those unpopular and undemocratic governments that are often the cause of the problem. Emergency relief should not be defined solely

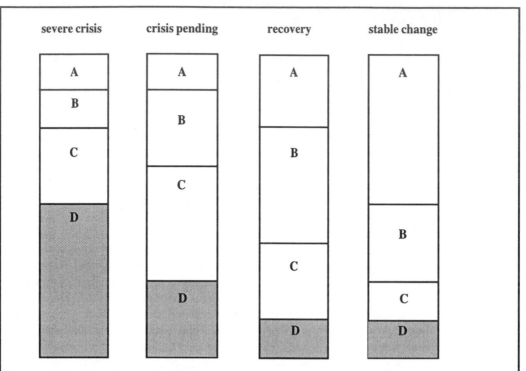

Figure 1: The changing emphasis of support

A represents support needs and roles related to income-generation, enterprise development, savings and credit, sustainable health and educations systems, environmental protection, capacity-building, institutional development; encouraging strategic alliances, increasing ability to dialogue with the state and undertake national and international lobbying, autonomisation, preparing withdrawal; the need to reinforce women's entitlements and rights to gain access to credit, health, education, legal protection; to promote and strengthen women's ability as individuals and as groups, and to develop networks and alliances with progressive agencies, legal services, etc.

B represents support needs and roles related to political stability, democracy at all levels, organising capacity, self-confidence, increased ability to deal with the next crisis, securing and re-starting production, rehabilitating or establishing infrastructure; broad-based training, network building, strengthening people's ability to make demands on government, building economic foundations for group development; the readjustment and renegotiation of women's roles and gender relations; promoting and strengthening women's groups and women in mixed groups.

C represents support and roles related to preparedness for possible crises, contingency planning, securing production, diversifying options, strengthening coping mechanisms; consolidating local control and management of resources by credit, training, support for organisational capacity; women as managers and consumers of a shrinking resource base, directly involved and supported in all projects.

D represents support needs and roles related to relief (e.g. provision of food, shelter, medicine), preservation of local culture, strengthening of local coping mechanisms, political protection, and lobbying, securing production; the provision of a liaison between community and external providers; thinking with community, 'being there', moral support, emphasis on life-enhancing principles, and avoiding dependency; women as guardians of family and culture, and as providers; protection, ensuring that, although vulnerable, women are not seen as victims.

as food aid or medicine, but should also include, among other things, such seemingly bizarre concepts as 'relief production', 'relief employment', 'relief income-generation' and 'relief institutional development'.

Turbulence and programming policy

There are clearly important differences between conflict and other disasters, such as famine, which may become critical in determining the response of the NGO community. Conflict is the playing out in violent form of political relations, which must be understood by NGOs if they are to avoid becoming part of the problem, rather than part of the solution. On the one hand, conflict can become structural or long-term in nature, and may lead to migrations which are far more massive and more long-term than those caused by natural crises (Macrae and Zwi 1992), which are usually less prolonged and less socially destructive. On the other hand, production and distribution, as well as restriction of movement and disruption of markets, are deliberately targeted during conflict. In such contexts, relief responses can easily be drawn into intensifying and prolonging conflict.

There are, however, similarities between the two types of situation. ACORD programmes in Mali, Somalia, and Uganda have followed a process which begins with a shrinking of development activities as the crisis looms, moves through a phase of consolidation or enters a holding pattern, before arriving at an assessment of what is possible in order to deal with long-term problems created by the crisis itself.[14] *Being there* and remaining there, even if no 'activities' are possible for a period, is important, for reasons which include moral support, playing a witness role, providing a symbolic presence, and enabling the programme staff to reassess what role they can play and what new opportunities they might take.

Capacities and vulnerabilities

The traditional approach to crisis or emergency tends to divide activities into pre-emergency, emergency, and post-emergency stages. However, the long-term nature of certain emergencies requires a long-term response that does not fit neatly into the relief/development boxes. As Anderson and Woodrow (1989) argue, we need to analyse **vulnerabilities**, which refer to the long-term factors which affect the ability of a community to respond to events, and which make it susceptible to crisis, in addition to **needs**, which refer to immediate requirements for survival or recovery from a crisis. Vulnerabilities (for example, the lack of access to land) precede disasters, contribute to their severity, impede response, and continue after the immediate crisis. Needs, by contrast, are generally shorter-term and immediate, such as the need for food or medicine.

Analysing vulnerabilities may prevent the urge for a 'return to normal', because, by exploring the factors that contributed to the crisis, it is seen that the previous situation involved vulnerabilities (or long-term trends) that may lead to future crises. In addition, it alerts relief workers to the potential for contributing to future vulnerabilities by their interventions. To avoid this, we also need to look at people's existing capacities, in order to know what strengths reside within a society, on which the future can be built. When a crisis becomes a disaster, a society's vulnerabilities are more noticeable than its capacities. However, we must understand both.

Local organisations and gender relations

An analysis of ACORD's experience (ACORD 1991) indicates that those programmes which have successfully adapted in times of crisis have been those that have invested in the long-term development of people and organisations with the skills, capacities, and above all confidence to propose and manage activities, as well as to sort out those conflicts among themselves which were generated by crisis. Thus ACORD has tended to address vulnerabilities from an organisational perspective, by strengthening existing groupings where possible. This has reinforced and extended local survival strategies, while also strengthening organisations' ability to negotiate with a wide range of external agencies, including distributors of emergency supplies. This allows local groups to interweave and enhance their own survival strategies with external support.

In times of unrest, new opportunities can arise, as the very crisis in which people find themselves forces them to work together. In Gulu (Uganda) and Somalia, this has enabled ACORD to work through community leaders and elders who had hitherto been seen as controlling power and influence, to the detriment of others. As crises subside, these opportunities can also start to disappear. A developmental approach to recovery is about using this period to bring about change, or consolidate gains made during the crisis. It is not about returning to the 'normality' or *status quo* which led to the crisis in the first place. For instance, gender relations are often radically changed during a crisis, sometimes for the better. In several countries in Africa (and elsewhere), there has been a tendency for women who played important roles during liberation struggles later to be expected to return to their pre-crisis roles. In Eritrea, the challenge is to preserve the gains made by women during the war, and to help them to resolve long-standing problems. Although societies seem not to act out of character in crises (inasmuch as cultural traits persist, sometimes in exaggerated form), new opportunities for change may emerge.

There is a danger that outside interventions may warp or destroy local institutions, by trying to determine things on their behalf. Providing information on experiences elsewhere, and reinforcing learning skills for groups to decide their own rules, structures, and procedures are preferable to deciding for others on the basis of ideal models. However, turbulence questions the notion of the institutionalisation of local structures and organisations. If they are to respond rapidly, do they not

also have to change rapidly, and possibly break up and re-form in new ways, as needs arise? Is the establishment of hierarchies, bureaucracies, and formal structures wise in these circumstances? Or should we be looking for much looser, informal alliances and networks?

Turbulence and management[15]

Rapid change requires sideways communication within organisations to become more commonplace. Hierarchical decision-making is suitable for routine problems that can be solved at a moderate pace. Agencies coping with rapid change cannot afford structures and procedures where decisions are allowed to wend their leisurely way up and down the hierarchy. Some have argued that this means the end of bureaucracy and the beginning of 'ad-hocracy', because the more rapidly the environment changes, the shorter the life-span of organisational form must become. Putting people in rigid slots and hierarchies becomes self-defeating, because it slows up responsiveness and adaptability. What is required are flexible organisational forms and alliances. This means organising into many semi-autonomous, semi-attached units, which can be spun off, and re-join if necessary, according to circumstances.

Turbulence can lead to managers spending a lot of time as trouble-shooters: rushing from one job to another, putting out fires, solving problems, or dealing with crises. Managers may concentrate on technical or organisational matters (programmes, representation, fund-raising) rather than on supervising, supporting, and managing staff. Managers must be prepared to give more time and priority to their management responsibilities; they need to get out of the 'trouble-shooting' mode, and spend more time on motivating their staff, training, facilitating discussions, and generating new initiatives. This does not mean forgetting crises, but instead seeing the managers' role as creating the capacity throughout the organisation or programme to cope with crises. It also means being able to provide staff with adequate training — and then delegate to them.

Turbulence and monitoring and evaluation

Alternative ways of working require new systems to monitor and evaluate them. We must learn to focus on a few manageable variables to measure what is important. Paradoxically, increasing complexity calls for the development of simpler systems. These should encourage participation and under-standing by everyone, and should support initiative-taking on the 'front line'. If systems are too complex, they thwart flexibility and slow up adaptability. Measurement should not be about collecting masses of data in compre-hensive base-line surveys. We need to keep things simple and visible. The test should be the existence of living, tangible, straightforward measures at the local level, *that people use in practice.*

In the private sector, Peters (1992) argues that the essential variables for monitoring and evaluation systems in turbulent contexts are simplicity of presentation, visibility of measurements, everyone's involvement, undistorted collection of primary data, straight-forward measurement of what is important, achievement of a sense of urgency, and perpetual involvement. What to collect, when to collect it, how to record it, and how to use it should be the province of 'front-line staff', who are properly informed about the interests of other stake-holders.

We can see how adaptable a programme or organisation is, and how well it might cope with rapid change, by asking:

• **How closely and how well an agency listens** to those it is trying to support and to those who fund them, thus increasing its 'porosity' to feedback. The point is that, if those being supported are being constantly listened to, agencies should be able to adapt more quickly. With increased listening to donors, the potential for misunderstandings

and bottle-necks can also be more rapidly identified.

• **How quickly and efficiently an agency learns from listening**, and from other organisations, and modifies its support accordingly. Translating listening into action, being open to change, constantly testing new ideas, learning from others and from past mistakes are all essential facets of responding to turbulence and rapid change.

• **How well an agency organises itself to promote learning and innovation** and so react appropriately to rapid change and turbulence. This demands organising in a way that allows well-trained staff to take decisions, that re-groups different interest-groups (donors, agencies, programme staff, and partners) to solve problems on the spot. This means more horizontal management and insist-ence on the primary focus being the 'front line', not one that puts bureaucratic hurdles in the way.

Our methods of monitoring and evaluation need to recognise that, although the process of enquiry is never-ending and subject to uncertainty, decisions must be reached in the mean time (Mearns 1991). As such, methods and indicators need to be not only appropriate in terms of the complexity and the cost involved, but also flexible and adaptable, and able to produce relevant, timely, accurate, and usable information that can satisfy different needs and interest groups.

Competition or collaboration?

Competition

NGOs' current preoccupation with strategic planning has thrown into sharp relief the competitive edge and rising market-share of those agencies involved in large-scale relief operations. This phenomenon is increasing as levels of available sub-contracting work rise for NGOs, especially in areas where bilateral and multilateral agencies are unable or unwilling to get involved.

For many NGOs who describe themselves as 'development' agencies, it is not the loss of market share *in itself* which is seen as the problem, but rather a perceived loss of profile and legitimacy, which in turn diminishes their ability to advocate and lobby against the factors which make relief necessary. It is assumed by some that their inability to act decisively and visibly compromises their relevance.

The result for many NGOs is a reworking of latent arguments about the assumed dichotomy between relief and development, which are now given added piquancy by strategic planning exercises based on analyses of strengths, weaknesses, opportunities, and threats, and market research. Eventually, NGOs' own survival strategies may become more important than those of the people they are trying to help (see Borton 1993 and Roche 1992).

There is increasing funding available for NGOs, mainly for sub-contracting deals, and mostly for emergency and rehabilitation work. The more opportunistic NGOs, which may be tempted to rely increasingly on this form of easily accessible funding, may start to change the public perception of NGOs in general, and so contribute to a gradual reduction in the range of roles which the sector has hitherto played. This may promote increasing competition between NGOs, lessening the sharing and collaboration between them, and increasing the concerns about their legitimacy and account-ability. It may also give rise to increased attempts by states to coordinate and control the proliferating number of NGOs, which in addition to complicating planning will be doing so with monies hitherto destined for Southern governments, and thus contributing to their 'institutional destruction' (see Farrington *et al.* 1993).

Many argue that NGOs' role is expanding — not because they have a comparative advantage, but because other 'channelling options are unavailable' (Fowler 1987). NGOs have sometimes become the only viable political alternative for channelling food and services in politically sensitive areas where governments and multilaterals are unable or unwilling to work. However, when NGOs implicitly become the private face of public policy, this abrogates the responsibility of governments to explain what their conditionality is, and defend their position publicly. NGOs themselves are not neutral channels, and are often fearful of alienating governments, both in donor countries and in recipient countries. The result is that there is pressure not to speak about root causes, which would embarrass governments and donors; and some would argue that NGOs' silence is thus being bought (Macrae and Zwi 1992).

Collaboration

New ways of thinking about and managing change implicitly challenge orthodox distinc-tions between relief and development, between what is normal and abnormal, between decent-ralisation and centralisation, and between diversity and unity. Above all, the assumed dichotomy between relief and development does not have to be managed alone. No single NGO can cover the whole range of emergency, development, and lobbying activities that are required. Turbulence calls for a much greater degree of coordination and collaboration between agencies operating at different levels *before, at the outset of, and during* a crisis. This has to be accompanied by a greater degree of trust between agencies, and a willingness to share problems and discuss solutions.

NGOs have to balance the dangers of developing an external, centralised, fixed menu of responses against those of decent-ralised parochialism, when local responses fail to draw on experience from elsewhere, or relate to those root causes which lie outside their area of influence. The need is for a more global view of development problems built upon *alliances* of competent agencies having wider experience and bringing *complementary* resources and skills to bear. Such broad-based alliances must include developmentally sensitive relief agencies as well as those human rights, peace, and lobbying organisations which are dealing with the wider issues.

Famine, conflict, and abuse of power and human rights are inextricably linked. NGOs have to ensure that the negative definition of rights favoured by Northern governments, which seeks the limitation of state power, is complemented by positive definitions which also speak of the obligations and responsibilities of national governments and the international community (Macrae and Zwi 1992). It is important that the human-rights card does not become another way of allowing Northern institutions to control aid allocations without changing *their* behaviour and *their* responsibilities. Human-rights monitoring needs to be integrated with the right to food and early warning systems. They should be based wherever possible on indigenous indicators and anecdotal material which can be translated into an analysis of need, vulnerability, and capacities. It is important that NGOs do not compound the problems created by the positions of Northern governments on human rights, by extracting the 'human rights' questions from the context of daily struggles for food and peace, and the forces which shape such struggles.

Ideas from the 'chaos' and 'complexity' debates in the natural sciences challenge NGOs to look more closely at change. We must understand the nature and source of change of which we are a part, rather than viewing it as an external force with which we have to cope. Instead of attempting to deal solely with events produced by different types of change, we must try to shape and guide the forces which produce such events, in order to change the nature of change itself.

Notes

1 ACORD is an international consortium of European and Canadian NGOs, working for long-term development in Africa.

2 *Crisis* is defined here as a critical juncture in a process at which a radical change becomes necessary. Thus a crisis represents a *period* of transformation, or transition when disaster threatens. *Disaster* is defined here as the situation that occurs when crisis outstrips the capacity of a society to cope with it.

3 Catastrophe theory emerged from the work of the nineteenth-century geologist Georges Cuvier, and was developed by a mathematician, René Thom, in the 1960s. In its broadest sense, catastrophe is the 'jump', or discontinuous change, from one state to another, such as from water to steam. It may be applied to literal disasters, but essentially catastrophe theory is a mathematical language created to describe any abrupt change.

4 Formal definitions of chaos made by mathematicians and physicists all include the notion of apparently random, irregular, but recurrent behaviour which is unpredictable, such as drought in the Sahel. They also refer to behaviour which amplifies small uncertainties, and frees analysis from 'the shackles of order and predictability' (Crutchfield quoted in Gleick 1987). It has also been argued that chaos is a set of ideas which allowed various disciplines to share a common and different way of looking at the world (Uphoff 1992), offering a way out of the compartmentalised view of science, and an end to the reductionist approach.

5 Some writers, such as Lewin (1993), suggest that chaos can be seen as a subset of complexity. If chaos theory was about showing how a few interactions could produce immensely divergent behaviour which looks random but is not, then complexity is about how interactions in non-linear systems may produce an emergent global order. Such ideas may be compared with the sociological notion of 'structuration' (Giddens 1981), which stresses a recursive relationship between the whole and the parts of a system. Morgan (1986) illustrates this with the example of a whirlpool, which gives the impression of stability, but has no existence outside the complex ebbs and flows of the river in which it exists.

6 See Uphoff 1992, Mearns 1991, Spooner 1991, and Chambers 1992.

7 See Gleick 1987, Stewart 1989, Woodcock and Davies 1978, and Lewin 1993.

8 In non-linear systems, small inputs can lead to dramatically large consequences. In weather, for example, this translates into the 'Butterfly Effect': the idea that a butterfly beating its wings today in the Far East can trigger storms over the USA at a later date. But the next time the butterfly flaps its wings, nothing might happen, which demonstrates the second feature of non-linear systems: small differences in initial conditions can lead to very different outcomes.

9 Looking at feedback encourages us to think in terms of 'loops not lines' (Morgan 1986). **Negative feedback** is where a change in a variable produces change in the opposite direction, and so leads to stability in a situation, i.e. more leads to less; while **positive feedback** multiplies change, so that more leads to more. The Club of Rome's project on the *Limits to Growth* made use of feedback models to show how world trends in population growth, pollution, and production could not be sustained if positive feedback systems did not have stabilising loops of negative feedback to 'damp' their effects.

10 Gleick (1987) notes that, to some physicists, chaos is a science of process rather than state, of *becoming* rather than *being*. Nature forms patterns. Some are orderly in space, but disorderly in time. Some exhibit the same structure at different scales, and some give rise to steady states. Pattern formation has become a branch of physics and of material sciences. Looking for patterns of change means asking why and how things are different, and looking for underlying trends of the whole, even if individual parts cannot be so defined.

11 Most complex systems contain what mathematicians call *attractors*, or stabilising points, around which change occurs, or states to which systems eventually settle. Lewin (1993) uses the examples of bands, tribes, chiefdoms, and states as stabilising points in terms of cultural evolution. He also notes that there is no necessary progression between these,

and that history demonstrates many cases of societies achieving 'higher' levels of organisation, and then falling back.

12 This term lacks precision, and is increasingly seen by ACORD as a less than helpful concept. It is questionable whether one can, or should, build sustainability on the basis of the existing relations between North and South, rich and poor, men and women, humanity and the environment. Hence ACORD prefers to think in terms of support which helps people to cope with, and promote, change.

13 The market can play a role in precipitating or in preventing famine. Cash support for vulnerable groups may improve entitlements, as well as stimulate demand. In addition, 'a reduction in livestock sales on the part of those receiving support could substantially benefit vulnerable livestock owners outside the relief system, by arresting impending collapse of livestock prices' (Drèze and Sen 1989, p. 102).

14 This is very similar to the process noted by Agerbak (1991), in a review of Oxfam's work in conflict areas.

15 Much of this section is unashamedly plagiarised from Peters (1987).

References

ACORD, 1991, 'Famine and Conflict in Africa: Challenges for ACORD', RAPP document No.4, ACORD.

Agerbak, L., 1991, 'Breaking the cycle of violence: doing development in situations of conflict', *Development in Practice*, 1/3: 151-8.

Anderson, M. and J. Woodrow, 1989, *Rising from the Ashes: Development Strategies in Times of Disaster*, Colorado: Westview Press.

Borton, J., 1993, 'Recent trends in the International Relief System', *Disasters*, 17/3: 187-201.

Brett, E.A., 1991, 'Recreating War-damaged Communities in Uganda: The Institutional Dimension', mimeo.

Chambers, R., *1992, Rural Appraisal: Rapid, Relaxed and Participatory,* IDS discussion paper No 311, Brighton: Institute for Development Studies.

Drèze, J. and A. Sen, 1989, *Hunger and Public Action*, Oxford: Oxford University Press.

Edwards, M. and D. Hulme (eds), 1992, *Making a Difference*, London: Earthscan.

Farrington, J., A. Bebbington, K. Wellard, and D.J. Lewis, 1993, *Reluctant Partners? NGOs, the State and Sustainable Agricultural Development*, London: Routledge.

Fowler, A., 1987, 'NGOs in Africa: Achieving Comparative Advantage in Relief and Micro-development?', paper presented at the conference on the role of indigenous NGOs in African Recovery and Development, Khartoum, Sudan.

Giddens, A., 1981, *A Contemporary Critique of Historical Materialism*, Berkeley: University of California Press.

Gleick, J., 1987, *Chaos: Making a New Science*, London: Cardinal.

Hettne, B., 1990, *Development Theory and the Three Worlds*, New York: Longman.

ICVA, 1991, *NGO Management*, April-June 1991 No. 21, Geneva.

Lewin, R., 1993, *Complexity: Life at the Edge of Chaos*, London: Dent.

Macrae, J. and A.B. Zwi, 1992, 'Food as an instrument of war in contemporary African famines', *Disasters*, 16/4: 299-321.

Mearns, R., 1991, *Environmental Implications of Structural Adjustment: Reflections on Scientific Method*, IDS discussion paper No. 284, University of Sussex.

Morgan, G., 1986, *Images of Organisation*, London: Sage.

Peters, T., 1987, *Thriving on Chaos: A Handbook for a Management Revolution*, London: Pan.

Peters, T, 1992, *Necessary Disorganisation for the Nano-Second Nineties,* London: Macmillan.

Roche, C., 1992, 'It's not the size that matters: ACORD's experience in Africa' in Edwards and Hulme (eds), 1992.

Spooner, B., 1991, *Fighting for Survival; Insecurity, People and the Environment in the Horn of Africa*, Geneva: IUCN.

Stewart, I., 1989, *Does God Play Dice?*, London: Penguin.

Uphoff, N., 1992, *Learning from Gal Oya; Possibilities for Participatory Development and Post-Newtonian Social Science*, Cornell University Press.

Watts, M., 1991, 'Entitlements or empowerment? Famine and starvation in Africa', *Review of African Political Economy*, 51:9-26.

Woodcock, A. and M. Davis, 1978, *Catastrophe Theory*, London: Penguin.

The author

Chris Roche conducted research in Burkina Faso from 1983 to 1985 on the role of NGOs. He was responsible for ACORD's West Africa programmes before becoming Head of the agency's Research and Policy Programme (RAPP). He is currently Programme Development Team Leader in Oxfam's Policy Department.

This article first appeared in *Development in Practice*, Volume 4, Number 3 (1994).

Breaking the cycle of violence:
doing development in situations of conflict

Linda Agerbak

Introduction

Since 1945, armed conflict has proved to be increasingly lethal for non-combatants. According to UN figures, there has been a steady rise in the proportion of recorded war-related deaths among civilians, up from 52 per cent in World War II to a shocking average of 84 per cent today (World Disarmament Campaign, 1989). The increase is due not just to new technology such as anti-personnel mines and fragmentation bombs. Indeed, most of those wars have been low-tech, compared with the recent Gulf War. More important is that they have nearly all been civil wars, in which both government and rebels have viewed whole sections of the population as the enemy. Such conflicts have functioned less like a duel between two armies and more like a massive abuse of the human rights of unarmed civilians. In the face of the resultant suffering and destitution — mainly for women, children, and the elderly — Northern and Southern NGOs have been challenged to respond with more than the usual food parcels. In order to respond to needs on the ground, some NGOs have also become drawn into human rights work, the treatment of trauma, support for conflict resolution, and campaigning for changes in official policy. These newer ways of working have on occasion challenged traditional concepts of relief and development, both within the NGO community and beyond.

The future needs of these war-torn societies also challenge NGOs to review their traditional role in supporting reconstruction. If the 1990s was a decade of increasing conflict, the 1990s may be a decade in which many warring societies will at last lay down the gun and pick up the hoe again. The end of 1989 marked the first year for 31 years that no new war had started (Sivard 1990). Indeed, a number of conflicts have already moved to a negotiated settlement, as in Namibia and Nicaragua, and others are trundling through the talk-talk fight-fight stage, as in Cambodia, Afghanistan, El Salvador, and Mozambique. Rebels in Somalia and Ethiopia have achieved outright military victories over the incumbent regime. What is clear in each case, however, is that, despite the end of one conflict, many issues remain to threaten these societies with a renewed round of violence in the future. This raises the question of what is the most effective role of NGOs in the immediate post-war phase.

At the reconstruction stage, the traditional assumption may be that the NGO role is to assist project holders to return to a previous baseline state of normality. For those fragmented and impoverished societies, however, the reality is that economic and social reconstruction cannot be divorced from questions of governance and political power. The fundamental task will be to break out of an on-going cycle of violence, as former enemies attempt to determine how they will relate to each other in the future. During the years of war, the message has been ingrained that the way to reclaim dignity and power is through violence, and that the way to settle disputes is by killing the opponent.

Added to this legacy of violence, growing population pressures on limited resources of land, water, and so on are creating new tensions. At current rates of population growth, there are 83 million more people to feed each year. Water resources are being diminished, and present trends indicate that almost a fifth of the earth's crop-land will have disappeared by the year 2000 (Oxfam, 1990). Options will inevitably become more limited, fears more acute, and conflict exacerbated. In the Sahel, these pressures are already leading to wars, as the Panos book *Greenwar* (Twose 1991) graphically describes.

The issue for NGOs then may be how to support the building of the 'civil society' — with responsive and accountable social organisations which render violence less likely. A second issue is how NGOs can use communications work to challenge unjust policies and practices which continue to fuel renewed conflict long after the peace settlement has been signed.

Background

In the sense of *dispute*, conflict is of course universal in the politics of family, community, and nation. In that sense, any dynamic human system is by nature a conflictive one, encompassing the play of opposing interests. The crux lies in how such conflict is managed. So long as the social and political processes provide channels for dialogue, participation, and negotiation (such as community development work seeks to foster), conflict plays a constructive role. Where such channels are blocked, and yet basic needs go unmet, then resentment and desperation build up. The outcome is protest, repression and violence.

The 'fortress' mentality

Such blockages are created when opposing interests are defined as vital, yet irreconcilable. Before such conflicts can be resolved, the dispute must be redefined to provide common ground for dialogue, negotiation, and accommodation. Such redefinition, however, is often resisted by those in charge, who, fearing change, retreat into political repression and fundamentalist ideology — the so-called 'fortress mentality'. Even where such fears can be mastered, objective factors such as poverty, debt, and increasing environmental pressure limit the options available to those seeking to manage the dynamic of conflict more constructively.

Polarisation and the fortress mentality are thought to be created and perpetuated by fear and insecurity, for example in regimes which lack political legitimacy, among insurgents caught up in a cycle of revenge for past grievances, or in social systems which are incapable of processing pressures for rapid change. Where change is blocked, a resolution of the impasse may require a change of leaders, a new constitution, or even a new generation who are able to redefine the issues. Sometimes war is the last desperate option for bringing about such change.

Poverty and conflict

The link between poverty and conflict is often mentioned, but seldom the nature of that link. Poverty is not by itself sufficient cause, as can be seen from poor countries not at war, such as Tanzania. The cause is not so much lack of resources *per se*, as injustice: social, economic, and political structures which maintain the dominance of an in-group at the centre of power, over an out-group at the periphery, to the extent of denying the most basic economic, social, and political rights. Johan Galtung has coined the term 'structural violence' to describe those patterns; others prefer the term 'structural injustice'. Apartheid is an obvious example. At the grass roots, such structures translate for the poor into landlessness, sub-subsistence wages, ill-health, illiteracy, and a lack of control over their own affairs. Such in-group/out-group structures operate at both local and national levels: through inequitable patterns of land tenure, exploitative labour practices, lack of access to education and health care, repressive security forces, a corrupt judiciary, and a muzzled press. Other structures and processes are international: the debt burden, unfair terms of trade, inappropriate aid, and coercive alliances.

The impact of such structures at grassroots level is that community organisations are harassed or suppressed, offices and vehicles are attacked, community leaders are intimidated, abducted, jailed, or killed. In reaction, the society polarises into opposing camps, and the political space for independent development groups rapidly closes. It is important to recognise the role of structural violence, and attendant human rights abuse, in provoking popular uprisings. These may at first be highly localised, in reaction to micro-incidents. If grievances are not addressed, however, and the State is unable effectively to repress opposition, the likelihood is that such local uprisings will coalesce over time into a wider insurgency.

The chaotic State

The above in-group/out-group analysis implies a strong centre and a weak periphery. But in other instances, the equation is reversed: weak organs of State power at the centre confront powerful groups at the periphery, resulting in a chaotic State, as in Lebanon, Afghanistan, and Uganda. Although many civil conflicts have been exacerbated by external rivalries, there are some where outside backers were arguably the determinant factor in destabilising a fledgling central government.

The role of NGOs

When societies turn to reconstruction, and where governments make a commitment to work for social justice, one option for NGOs may be to work with various branches of government to strengthen their capacity for good governance. Northern NGOs may also have a role to play by liaising with their own governments on the need for reconstruction aid to include bilateral aid for democratisation and human rights. NGOs in Canada, the Netherlands, and the Scandinavian countries have led the way on this (Tomasevski, 1989).

Impact of conflict

Although war is often seen in terms of death and destruction, the reality of it for people living in poverty produces a much broader range of economic and social effects, even for people living far from the actual shooting. Spreading violence makes itself felt first in economic terms: closed health posts, absent teachers, empty shops and markets. It also means food shortages, due to the disruption of farming, transport and trade. Rural subsistence economies are deliberately undermined: crops are plundered or burnt by soldiers, farmers are maimed by mines, forced conscription diverts productive labour. Economic disintegration leads to a lack of opportunities for income generation. Many skilled managers and technicians use their resources in order to flee; those who choose to remain become targets of repression. Eventually war may lead to economic collapse and destitution. Where this coincides with the failure of rain, and the deliberate use of food denial as a strategy of war, the result is famine, as in Ethiopia, Sudan, Somalia, northern Uganda, Mozambique, and Angola (Duffield, 1991).

Social costs are also high. Military operations cause the displacement of families and the disintegration of communities. Poor people find themselves caught between security forces on the one hand and insurgents on the other. The deliberate use of terror to cow the population has taken its toll on thousands of non-combatants in many conflicts. The survivors carry nightmare memories of attack, family separation and loss, displacement from their land/community, and perhaps abduction, rape, and torture. Psychiatrists speak of the tendency for individuals, including health professionals, to withdraw from the survivors of violence (Goldfeld, 1988). Where trauma has affected many people in a community, it may be difficult to reknit the trust and social cohesion necessary for post-war recovery. NGOs are still at the beginning of their search for an appropriate and culturally sensitive role in response to widespread war trauma among refugees and the displaced.

Development out of conflict?

It is a truism that the demoralisation, impoverishment, chaos, and social breakdown created by war damages a society's longer-term capacity for development. But the experience of Zimbabwe, Nicaragua, Eritrea, and South Africa shows that the conflict may also create new social structures and ways of working, and the political solution it brings forth may open up new possibilities for development.

How programmes evolve: relief and development

The high-profile disaster relief programme — with its dramatic public appeal, rapid assessment, and special funding procedure — conveys the unspoken message that the appropriate NGO response to conflict is an emergency programme. Despite many years of war, such palliative, 'short-term' emergency projects still account for the greater part of NGO response to conflict in Ethiopia, Sudan, Uganda, Angola, and Mozambique. Such work, however valuable it has been in relieving immediate suffering, has made little impact on the underlying problems and causes of the conflict; food packages, which are an appropriate response for natural disasters, are inappropriate as the *sole* response to conflict. Careful assessment is needed before any intervention is made, to ensure that, at a minimum, the NGO response will not exacerbate the underlying problems and causes of the conflict. Moreover, where attention is focused on the process as well as the inputs of relief, opportunities can be found to empower local groups and beneficiaries, particularly women.

Apart from the emergency response, NGOs can become more effective across the board in responding to conflict when they understand how programmes grow and change, as problems and opportunities are identified and addressed. Four stages can be discerned: damage, crisis, consolidation, and recovery. In the first, emerging violence causes the existing development programme to be cut back. In the

second, intensifying violence creates a turning point when development is shelved and short-term relief programmes spring up. In the third, programmes acquire 'development' characteristics: i.e. longer-term planning, belated socio-economic assessments, democratisation, institution-building; technical training; increasing self-reliance. And finally, when a peace settlement is reached, there is the task of recovery.

Stage 1: damage — the shrinking development programme

In countries where long-term development programmes are gradually overtaken by conflict, the tendency has been to persevere with development in the face of increasing political polarisation, violence, unpredictability, and economic decline. NGOs try to keep vulnerable community projects alive and independent. In the growing atmosphere of suspicion, it is also important, but increasingly difficult, to maintain space for NGOs to talk to each other.

Stage 2: crisis — from development to relief

A turning point comes when intense violence and impoverishment force NGOs to reassess the aims and style of their programmes. Development projects are shelved. Project holders gear up to meet urgent new conflict-related needs, but they work with a sense of doing a holding operation until things improve. No long-term plans are possible. As one development worker stated of Lebanon in 1984, 'What is becoming more and more clear is the intrinsic absurdity of trying to initiate development in a society that is crumbling at every level and in every way, whether economically, politically, socially, culturally or morally.'

Stage 3: Consolidation — doing development in conflict

Over time, the conflict settles into a pattern, and project holders gain experience. Both funding NGOs and project holders take stock, which leads to the application of more stringent standards of project assessment and greater commitment to a focus on poverty, participative structures, and gender awareness.

As a result, criticisms of hastily designed projects begin to surface. Evaluations and reviews take place. Project holders undertake institutional development, and professionalise their approach with appropriate training and staffing. Emergency and recovery programmes give way to social organisation and communications, with a view to addressing the longer-term problems created by conflict, and perhaps even some of the causes of it.

In Lebanon, for example, where sectarian fragmentation was a major cause of the conflict, an NGO might choose to work with non-sectarian partners, and fund cultural and youth work with Arab groups, to lay the foundations for a more united country. Where minority rights have been a source of discord, as among the indigenous peoples of Guatemala and the Atlantic Coast of Nicaragua, it would be possible to support work to strengthen cultural identity and reduce isolation. Where Northern factors have been important, campaigning and networking come into play, as with Cambodia, Nicaragua, and southern Africa.

Stage 4: Planning for peace

Once a settlement is within reach, attention needs to be directed to building the peace. The concept of recovery should be broadened, to include not just the rural economy's need for such inputs as seeds and tools, but also strategies of empowerment and advocacy that will tackle the longer-term cycle of violence. These are some of the issues involved in planning for peace:

• The difficulties of going from a relief approach, based on inputs, to a development approach, based on self-sufficiency. The habit of dependency is so strongly ingrained that NGOs may have to close projects and open new ones with other project holders.

• Strategies for avoiding going operational, such as networking in advance of a settlement in order to identify possible project partners.

• Increased needs for training in negotiation skills, as former enemies are thrown together, and the opposition gains a political role at all levels, as in Namibia, South Africa and Nicaragua.

• The need for a national development plan, policy, and structures, as in Namibia and Cambodia.

• The importance for NGOs of maintaining independent space. The current government may not be the same as in a few years' time, and NGOs which have become identified with one side or another may find themselves marginalised as political power begins to shift.

• The need for active lobbying for official reconstruction aid, to cover not only economic measures but also democratisation and human rights work.

Factors blocking the evolution of programmes

Reviewing the experience of development agencies suggests that it is three or more years before any conflict-related programme progresses beyond crisis into an effort to address development in conflict. The question must be whether NGOs might arrive at such a consolidation earlier.

Why do NGOs report such difficulty in moving towards programmes that tackle the deeper problems and causes of conflict? What are the blocking factors? Certainly a sustained high level of violence; also perhaps the lack of suitable partners.

But there may also be internal NGO factors blocking such change. Where a rigid distinction is made between relief and development, programmes may be slow to evolve. Staff selection may also be a problem: staff most appropriate for emergency relief situations may not have development experience. Staff isolation may be another block. For some agencies, the ease and attraction of fundraising for high-profile short-term relief activities may influence interventions. Agencies must ask themselves how they can overcome these internal blocks.

New staff, outside visits, and external reviews often act as catalysts in the evolution of the programme. If sufficiently prepared, regional conferences can promote further reflection and cross-fertilisation. It has also been suggested that conflict-related programmes should be reviewed more frequently.

Defining aims

While high-profile conflict emergencies, such as the displacement of Kurds in Iraq in 1991, create their own momentum, some Northern NGOs have become wary of starting relief work in a new country where they have not been working in development. Others, however, welcome the opportunity to go into a new country, where a relief programme may later lead to development work.

It is not enough to respond to a situation of conflict with unquestioning efforts to supply water, food, and shelter. NGOs must also make an effort to analyse the roots of the conflict and the problems it creates for the poor, and from this to identify the NGO's most effective role, with a coherent programme that addresses the key issues. Such an analysis cannot of course take place without a working knowledge of the culture and a good grasp of political, social, and economic factors. Longer-term objectives developing from this analysis may include securing the food supply, enabling economic, social, and environmental recovery, supporting the efforts of the displaced to return home, opposing abuses of human rights, empowering communities to resist repression, affirming their cultural identity, healing social fragmentation, addressing the need for peace, or campaigning against certain official policies.

Limited options

The options open to NGOs will be limited, however, not only by the intensity of violence, but also by the general level of economic and social development, the political climate, and the presence of other agencies. To understand this helps to answer the nagging question of why programme profiles are so different in Central America from those in Sudan or Mozambique. In areas where suitable local organisations exist, and popular education is generating a struggle for empowerment and social and economic justice, donor NGOs will find opportunities to move their programme, as advocated above, beyond the relief stage. Thus NGO interventions would include work to strengthen popular organisations, human rights, development work with refugees and displaced people, and communications work to promote a critical analysis of the situation.

Such options may not, regrettably, exist in many other conflict situations. Often there are few independent organisations to work with; widespread violence impedes operations; and the climate makes human rights work and advocacy difficult. The only option then might well be a holding action in the context of a rolling crisis.

Conclusion

The difficulties and dilemmas described above, however, must not hold NGOs back from reflecting on their approach to conflict. Immense amounts of public money go into conflict-related aid, and NGOs have a duty to make good use of it, and to be accountable for doing so.

The most pressing need is for conflict-related work to be reviewed more frequently, and for concerned staff to be given the opportunity to stand back from their crisis-ridden programmes in order to reflect. This in turn implies more resources put into staff training, to exchange the best experience among relief and development workers, to extend thinking about the aims of such programmes in conflict, and the options for doing development in specific conflict situations. A way must be found to train relief staff in rapid socio-economic assessment, and particularly in the needs of women.

Specifically, there is a need to share thinking, research, and experience on four crucial matters:

- possible programme options in cases where traditional work in conflict zones actually reinforces repressive governments;

- working with human rights organisations in conflict;

- the appropriate NGO role in the treatment of war trauma, in both relief and development situations;

- in post-war situations, how to develop in-country capacity to manage future conflict more constructively, perhaps through organisations which can offer training to community groups, labour unions, security forces, youth workers, health personnel, and local government employees.

Finally, agencies need to be more open, to share experiences and dilemmas of working in conflict. In the context of the end of the Cold War, they have an important role to play in helping to build civil societies which have the resources to break the historical cycle of violence.

References and bibliography

Amnesty International, 1990, *Annual Report*, London: Amnesty International.

Chomsky, Noam, 1991, 'The Struggle for Democracy in a Changing World', paper presented at a Catholic Institute for International Relations conference on 'Negotiating for Change', London.

Curle, Adam, 1986, *In the Middle*, Oxford: Berg.

Duffield, Mark, 1991, *War and Famine in Africa*, Oxford: Oxfam Publications.

Goldfeld, Anne et al., 1988, 'The physical and psychological sequelae of torture', *Journal of the American Medical Association*, 259:2725-9.

Keen, David, 'A disaster for whom? Local interests and international donors during famine among the Dinka of Sudan', *Disasters* 15/2: 151-65.

Miall, Hugh, 1989, 'How Conflicts Were Resolved 1945-1985', Oxford: Oxford Research Group.

Oxfam, 1990, *Oxfam and the Environment*, Oxford: Oxfam Publications.

Sadruddin Aga Khan, 1981, *Study on Human Rights and Massive Exoduses*, New York: UNESCO Commission on Human Rights.

Sivard, Ruth, 1990, *World Military and Social Expenditures 1989*, New York: World Priorities.

Tomasevski, Katerina, 1989, *Development Aid and Human Rights*, London: Pinter.

Twose, Nigel (ed.), 1991, *Greenwar*, London: Panos.

World Disarmament Campaign, 1989, 'Disarmament Facts 70: Armament and Disarmament: Questions and Answers', London: World Disarmament Campaign.

Wallace, Tina, 1990, 'Refugee Women, Their Perspectives and Our Responses', paper presented at a Refugee Consortium, Institute of Social Studies, The Hague.

The author

Linda Agerbak worked in South East Asia for six years as a development consultant and journalist, before being commissioned by Oxfam (UK and Ireland) to undertake a study of the NGO response to armed conflict. She has recently helped to establish Cardiff Mediation, a neighbourhood conciliation project in Wales.

This article was originally published in *Development in Practice*, Volume 1, Number 3, in 1991.

Famine and human rights

Alex de Waal

Where we stand

Famine has often been regarded as an act of God, and, no matter how many times academic students of famine say otherwise, this attitude seems to remain well-implanted in the minds of politicians, journalists, and the general public. These people like to believe that famine characteristically follows a natural disaster such as a drought or flood.

In the 1970s, at the time of the famines in the West African Sahel, Ethiopia, and Bangladesh, the Marxists began to propound an alternative view. With regard to Africa, their popular slogan was 'drought is not famine'. They identified famine as the result of long-term socio-economic processes which render rural populations impoverished and vulnerable to climatic shocks which would otherwise have caused no undue distress. Specifically they blamed the growth of capitalism under the aegis of the colonial state for supplanting indigenous social and economic structures. *Silent Violence* is the name of the best-known study in this field.[1] This approach has received a good deal of criticism lately, on the grounds that there are many famines which do not conform to this model, and that the record of peripheral capitalism in Africa is not one wholly of loss. But it remains undeniable that socio-economic processes are central to an understanding of famine, and that, in the extreme, they can cause famine. Starvation, if it occurs, is the outcome of long processes of marginalisation and impoverishment.

However, though brutal, the workings of such socio-economic systems do not fall obviously under the mandate of human rights organisations, and Marxists do not tend to turn to human rights organisations for assistance with analysis or action.

The point of entry of human rights concerns into the issue of famine has been located elsewhere entirely. It has centred round an entirely different paradigm of man-made famine: the deliberate denial of relief food to civilians in a war zone, usually with the aim of starving them into submission. This does occur and is important, and certainly should be of concern to human rights organisations.

A much more profitable approach to the issue lies somewhere in between these two angles. Instead of trying to marry the two, it is better to start from scratch in our understanding of what famine is (in Africa), and how human rights concerns are important to that.

Understanding famine in Africa

Famines in Africa are not what English speakers typically think they are. This is not the place for a long academic digression into different definitions of famine, but several points need to be made.

One point is that, while the English definition of 'famine' implies mass starvation, most of the famines which we diagnose in Africa and in which we give assistance are not episodes of mass starvation. Death rates remain comparatively low (perhaps 4 or 5 per cent per year), and most deaths that do occur are caused by infectious diseases. Outright starvation is extremely rare. These are disasters certainly, but not the apocalypses commonly predicted in the press. African definitions of famine, by contrast, centre on suffering in general, and differentiate between famines of different degrees of severity.

The different degrees of famine can be represented by the metaphor of a thermometer. The famine becomes more intense as the temperature goes down: at 'dearth' we are very cold; 'famines that kill' start at freezing; and 'famines that starve' are well into the degrees below zero.

The second point to make is that the difference between a mild famine and a severe one can be very great. Table 1 extends the metaphor of the thermometer, assuming that the 'temperature' is directly proportional to the death rate, and charts where some well-known famines fall (the precise figures should not be taken too seriously).

The death rates in camps are always elevated compared with those among the general population (typically they are five times more), so camp figures have not been included, except where the entire population has been forced to live in camps or camp-like conditions. (This held in part for both of the last two cases.) By way of comparison, the worst refugee camps and famine shelters in Ethiopia in 1984 scored about minus 60.

With the part-exception of the Sahel famine, all these are famines that kill. Starvation *per se* begins to figure at about minus 10, after which famines become much worse rather quickly. This underlines the need to be very careful in using the term 'famine', and to use special discretion concerning the word 'starvation'.

What is striking about these cases is that the first six were famines that occurred in peace time (excepting Ethiopia, of which see more below), whereas the last four were, in one way or another, accompanied by violence, forced removal of populations, and counter-insurgency strategies that involved gross violations of human rights.[2]

Famine coping strategies: Sudan 1984-5[3]

It is interesting to compare the people of western Sudan in 1984-5 and the southern Sudanese displaced to western Sudan in 1988. The death rates among the latter were, for a few months, 60 times as bad as among the former (about ten times as bad as the worst camp populations of the former). Yet the two famine-stricken populations lived in the same area, and there was much more food available in that area in 1988 than there was in 1984.

The key difference between the two was that in 1984-5 the drought-stricken people of western Sudan were able to pursue their coping strategies. This was by far the most important factor in the survival of the great majority of the population during that famine. If we take the population of Darfur region, during the two years of the famine, the food grown by the farmers themselves accounted for no more than 35 per cent of their food-consumption needs. Food aid met only 10 per cent. The balance was met partly by going hungry, but mostly by resourcefulness and ingenuity. The 'coping

Table 1

West African Sahel, 1970–3	minus one degree
Ethiopia 1987, Ethiopia 1990/1	minus 1–2
Western Sudan, 1984–5	minus 3
Northern Ethiopia 1973	minus 4
Red Sea Hills, Sudan, 1985	minus 5
Northern Ethiopia, general, 1984	minus 6
Karamoja, Uganda, 1980	minus 9
Northern Ethiopia, worst areas, 1984	minus 10
Resettlement camps, Ethiopia	minus 15
Displaced southern Sudanese, 1988	down to minus 240

strategies' followed, in approximate order of importance, were as follows:

- eating wild foods ;
- migrating to work as hired labour on farms;
- petty trade and casual work in towns;
- selling animals;
- borrowing;
- obtaining charity from richer relatives and neighbours;
- and a host of other activities.

These coping strategies were, cumulatively and in aggregate, at least five times as important as food aid in helping people to survive the famine. (We could also point out that the food aid came late and went mostly to the wrong people, so that for the really poor it provided in fact only the last ten per cent at most.)

In addition, farmers were able to keep their land, and use it. The famine finished in late 1985 with a good harvest. But this harvest did not just come from nowhere: the crops were planted and tended by the famine 'victims' themselves, right throughout the last and worst months of hunger. Similarly, many herders finished the famine with some animals, which they had carefully fed and watered throughout the long months of drought and hunger: animals they could have sold at any time to buy food, or consumed themselves. Not only did almost all the people survive, but they survived with the economic base of their future livelihood intact, so that they could return to self-sufficiency when the famine was over.

Famine and counter-insurgency: Sudan 1988[4]

The difference between this picture of tenacity and survival and the cataclysm of 1988 among the displaced southerners is due to the counter-insurgency methods of the Sudan government. In 1984 there was no war in western Sudan. The non-democratic nature of the government (characterised by unaccountable politicians and the absence of a free press) meant that the government could ignore the developing famine and do nothing to initiate relief programmes. But it did nothing to destroy rural people's livelihoods or to prevent them from following their coping strategies. In the south, in 1988, it did precisely these things.

Government action, through the army and the militias, had two main effects. First, it destroyed the productive base of Dinka society. Land was made unusable through the threat of raiding or the poisoning of wells, and in some areas through the indiscriminate dissemination of land mines. Animals were killed or stolen. People were forcibly removed from their farms and pastures and taken north or driven to seek refuge in local towns. Commerce was destroyed or disrupted.

Second, action by the army and militias prevented people from following their coping strategies. By far the most important of these actions was the prevention of free movement. This ruled out the possibility of labour migration, of collecting wild foods in the forests, of travelling to seek help from relatives or to sell assets in markets. Most of the survival strategies so important in 1984–5 depended on movement, and a ban on movement was tantamount to a sentence of death. People's only chance was to migrate out of the counter-insurgency zone altogether — a trek of 1,000 miles to Khartoum or Ethiopia. Other actions which disrupted or prevented coping strategies included preventing people working for money, preventing them collecting wild foods, preventing free commerce (by stopping markets or fixing prices), and, lastly, preventing access to food aid and medical assistance.

Thus we see that the obstruction of food aid, while it was important, was only part of a larger picture of abuses. If the obstruction of food aid — the last ten per cent — is of concern to a human rights organisation, then the prevention of the strategies which would otherwise have provided the first 90 per cent is also of concern.

Ethiopia

Ethiopia is notorious for its famines, and the Ethiopian government is notorious for its violations of human rights. *[Editor's note: this article was written before the fall of the Mengistu regime.]* The two facts are closely linked, though Ethiopia shows a slightly different pattern of famine-creating abuses from that in Sudan.

Some of the practices in Ethiopia which have turned hardship into famine and famine into mass starvation include the following:

- forced removals and displacement by resettlement, villagisation, and military campaigns;
- requisitioning of produce by the army;
- destruction of animals, crops, and agricultural implements by the army;
- the fixed price and quota system of procurement from peasants by the Agricultural Marketing Corporation;
- fear of moving to the towns by peasants afraid of conscription and forced removal;
- heavy taxation;
- bans on free commerce, and bombing of markets in rebel areas preventing commerce;
- diversion, obstruction, and destruction of food aid.

Some of these government actions are associated with counter-insurgency methods, and some are associated with centralised totalitarian state planning, without any checks on it. In general, the famines in the north of the country have been associated mainly with counter-insurgency, and in the south with bad planning ruthlessly implemented. Tigray, perhaps the worst-hit region in 1984, suffered from the most brutal counter-insurgency campaign, notably the seventh and eighth offensives of the Ethiopian army, and fiercely enforced bans on movement and commerce. Wollo, hit nearly as badly, suffered both counter-insurgency measures and disastrous agricultural policies.

These factors were of great importance in creating famine in 1984. They were much less important in Tigray province of Ethiopia in 1987 and (especially) 1989/90, despite the greater attention given to the war by the international media. This is because in 1987 the rebel fronts controlled a much larger area of the country, and so the government policies and army strategies had much less of an impact. By 1989 the government had been expelled from the whole of Tigray. In contrast to 1984, therefore, there was very little fighting and no governmental controls. The effect of the war was to cut off Tigray from most foreign aid. This was presented as a disaster for the people. However there is no doubt that the people of Tigray would rather have no aid and no government controls or attacks, than aid and a government presence.

Political freedoms and famine[5]

When famine looms in a society without a free press and democratic political institutions, there is little pressure on the government to do anything about it. On average, Africans eat more than Indians. But India has not suffered famine for more than forty years, and this can largely be attributed to the free press and adversarial politics of the country. (The other factor in India's success is the government's willingness to intervene in the economy to support the poor in times of threatening famine.)

The occurrence of the great famine of 1958-61 in socialist China has been attributed in part to the lack of information about the crisis, deriving from Mao's 'Great Leap Forward' and the strict censorship that entailed. Politicians who were aware of the crisis were unable to publicise it or organise to represent the interests of the vulnerable people, on account of the authoritarian political system. Similarly, the occurrence of the famine of 1984-5 in capitalist Sudan can be attributed in part to the strict controls on the press and government actions against groups that tried to organise on behalf of the stricken people. The Sudan government did not want to discourage private investment by admitting to the embarrassment of a famine.

These examples demonstrate that political rights — to information, to free association, to representation — are important in fighting famine, irrespective of the economic system.

They are important in two ways. One, the free flow of information means that the powerful people in society know about the plight of the poor. Two, the rights of association and representation mean that the poor are able, through adversarial civil politics, to press for their material needs to be met. These rights are of direct concern to human rights organisations, both because they are prized in themselves, and because their violation makes a poor country vulnerable to famine.

Economic freedoms and famine[6]

Some of these famine-creating measures in Ethiopia, such as the pricing and procurement policy of the Agricultural Marketing Corporation, or the licensing system for small traders, do not fall under the brief of a human rights organisation in an obvious way. They are violations of economic freedoms, which are not normally seen as basic human rights. In normal times these would be of concern only to economic policy makers and free-market ideologues. However, when rural people are no longer living in normal times but have been pushed to the margin of survival, such matters can mean the difference between life and death.

How are we to bring a human rights analysis to bear on these government actions? One approach is to take economic freedoms seriously. The accounts of Sudan in 1988 and Ethiopia imply that a *laissez faire* policy of respecting economic freedoms will help to prevent famine. In these cases it certainly would. But in other cases this does not hold. Socialist countries are on the whole better than capitalist ones at overcoming hunger. Capitalism allows for the exercise of economic freedoms by wealthy people during famine, such as profiteering in the grain market, or buying up land or assets cheaply, which help to make matters worse for the poor. In capitalist Sudan, merchants continued to export grain during the famines of 1984 and 1988.

When famines do strike socialist countries, they tend to be particularly bad. People in a centrally planned economy are forced to rely on the state, and when that fails, they have few alternatives for assisting themselves. Capitalist countries may be more often prone to famine, but these are less likely to degenerate into severe famines, because the system allows for greater local-level coping strategies.

We cannot make a strong case for a human rights critique of socialism on the grounds that when it fails, it results in a particularly severe kind of famine.

We should also note that the denials of economic freedom in Sudan in 1988 occurred as the result of a counter-insurgency strategy by a capitalist government. Central socialist planning played no part. Moreover, in Ethiopia, while the disastrous economic policies of the government (criticised by socialists and capitalists alike) caused much impoverishment and misery, even famine, the severe famines were associated with systematic violence. Some of this violence was perpetrated during counter-insurgency campaigns, and some during the brutal implementation of programmes of social engineering.

Economic freedoms are therefore not linked to famine in a simple way. In certain cases, the denial of economic freedoms can be critical in turning a mild famine into a severe one, but in many cases planned economies provide more food to the poor than free-market ones. The point of concern for a human rights organisation should be not so much the fact that an economic freedom is being abrogated, but that the result of the action is the creation of acute misery — severe famine or starvation. The ethics are essentially utilitarian. (Like utilitarianism, an approach centred on material rights is more powerful when analysing deprivation and misery than when analysing fulfilment and happiness.) In addition, we may note that this typically occurs when a government uses violence or coercion.

Counter-insurgency famines

The very worst famines are created by counter-insurgency operations. These are of concern to human rights organisations in several respects:

1 Counter-insurgency operations that create famine usually involve systematic and widespread violations of basic human rights, including mass killing and looting.

2 Counter-insurgency operations involve severe restrictions on economic activities, including the ability to use productive resources (i.e. grow food) and the freedoms to move, trade, etc.

3 In counter-insurgency operations the deliberate creation of famine is often an aim of the government.

Conclusion

Famine is an issue in which material rights and liberal human rights come together. This is an important fact that has often been missed, and the ethic of apolitical humanitarianism that informs most of the discussion of famine contributes to its being overlooked. The apolitical humanitarian approach — providing food aid to all without regard to the political consequences of this — has also proved manifestly inadequate for solving the problem of famine. This is because food relief provides at best the 'last ten per cent' which enables famine-stricken people to survive, and the provision of this relief, no questions asked, may assist governments in inflicting the damage that creates famine in the first place.

The analysis of this paper implies a completely different approach to famines, particularly those associated with counter-insurgency operations. If a government is required to cease perpetrating the abuses which are creating the famine (or are turning a mild famine into a severe one and thus raising death rates tenfold or more), this will have far more impact than providing food relief. Specific recommendations may include allowing free movement of people, allowing people to gather wild foods and seek work, letting 'commercial' food move freely across battle lines, ceasing raids against civilian villages, and stopping forced requisitioning of crops.

In addition, if rights to information, association, and political representation are respected, famine is likely to be averted in the first place.

Such measures would represent real medicine for famine, rather than the current band-aid approach which conceals the wounds, only to allow them to fester.

Notes

1 Watts, M. (1983), *Silent Violence: Food, Famine and Peasantry in Northern Nigeria* (University of California Press).
2 The theoretical underpinnings of this argument are presented in a paper by the present author: 'A re-assessment of entitlement theory in the light of the recent famines in Africa', *Development And Change*, Vol. 21: 469-90 (1990).
3 This section is based on Chapters 4 to 7 of A. de Waal: *Famine That Kills: Darfur, Sudan, 1984-1985* (Oxford: Oxford University Press).
4 This section is based on Chapter 4 of *Denying 'The Honour Of Living', Sudan: A Human Rights Disaster* (Africa Watch, March 1990).
5 *Starving In Silence: A Report On Famine And Censorship* (Article 19, April 1990).
6 See J. Dreze and A. Sen: *Hunger And Public Action* (Oxford: Oxford University Press, 1990).

The author

Alex de Waal was awarded a D.Phil by Oxford University for his thesis, published in 1989 by Oxford University Press under the title *The Famine That Kills: Darfur, Sudan, 1984-1985*. He has worked for Oxfam as a consultant in Tigray, and is currently the Co-Director of African Rights.

This article was first published in *Development in Practice* Volume 1, Number 2 (1991).

'Dancing with the prince':
NGOs' survival strategies in the Afghan conflict

Jonathan Goodhand with Peter Chamberlain

Introduction

In the era of democratisation and good governance, NGOs have become the donors' 'favoured child', with access to growing resources and influence (Edwards and Hulme, 1995). They are viewed both as 'market actors' which are more efficient and cost-effective than governments, and as the agents of democratisation, an integral part of a thriving civil society (Korten 1990, Clark, 1991). Official donors show their support for the economic and political roles of NGOs in what has been called the 'New Policy Agenda' by channelling money through them (Edwards and Hulme, op. cit.). As one USAID official put it: 'We get a double bang for our buck that way' (Larmer, 1994). Underpinning this consensus is the presumption that political democracy and socio-economic development are mutually reinforcing. The State, market, and civil society — which, following Korten (1990), we shall refer to as *prince, merchant* and *citizen* — are related in a series of virtuous circles. A basic tenet of 'NGO lore' is that NGOs promote and strengthen civil society, and thus subject the prince and merchant to greater public accountability.

There is, however, an element of triumphalism in the discourse about the New World Order, and the belief that NGOs are 'part of the warp and weft of democracy' (Larmer, op. cit.). Such words ring hollow in a world characterised by instability, fragmentation, and deepening poverty. Far from 'democratising development', NGOs are often the providers of palliatives to competing factions in conflict (Slim, 1994). Rather than promoting accountability, NGOs are perhaps 'dancing to the tune of the prince', whether the prince is a government, an insurgency movement, or a local war lord. We should challenge the assumptions underpinning the mythology about NGOs; and donors should base their actions on a realistic assessment of NGOs' capabilities, rather than on the suppositions of 'NGO lore'.

Background to the Afghan conflict

The end of the Cold War has not meant the end of history, as Fukayama suggested (Rupesinghe, 1994). Far from being a 'New World Order', today's world is characterised by a dangerous disorder, in which political instability is endemic.[1]

The Afghan war is a potent example of contemporary conflicts, often described as 'complex political emergencies' (CPEs), which are characterised by combinations of multiple causes, such as civil and ethnic conflicts, famine, displacement, disputed sovereignty, and a breakdown of national government. The Afghan conflict resulted from a complex mix of factors, caused by years of bad development, Cold War politics, militarisation, and tribal and ethnic schisms. It thus highlights many critical issues: the breakdown of the nation-state, ethnicity, fundamentalism, nationalism, displacement, sovereignty, and the role of humanitarian agencies.

CPEs are not temporary crises after which society returns to normal; they have long-term, structural characteristics and result from the failures of development. By the mid-1970s, Afghanistan had become a schizophrenic society: an urban elite whose idea of a strong, unified State was at odds with the tribal and ethnic loyalties of the predominantly rural population. From these contradictions arose the socialist and the Islamicist movements. Both were based on the 'myth of revolution', and it was the clash between these ideologies which became the catalyst for the conflict.

The 'Lebanonisation' of Afghanistan

The Afghan conflict was characterised by the implosion of the nation-state, the development of predatory political movements and war economies, and the erosion of structures within civil society. Macrae and Zwi (1992) describe the deliberate targeting of production and distribution, as well as restriction of movement and disruption of markets, in the context of Africa. In Afghanistan, rural subsistence economies were deliberately destroyed by Soviet forces during the 1980s, and terror was used to cow the population, one third of whom were displaced to Iran and Pakistan.

The withdrawal of Soviet troops in 1988 did not signal an end to the conflict. A process of 'Lebanonisation' (Roy, 1989) followed, in which the contradictions within the resistance movement re-surfaced. The conflict thus mutated from a counter-insurgency war with an ostensibly ideological basis into one characterised by war-lordism and banditry. The overall picture is one of fluidity and turbulence; alliances are constantly shifting, and violent conflict is interspersed with fragile peace. Competing 'princes' have a vested interest in the continuation of disorder; where their fortunes are based on coercion and, increasingly, on the opium trade, they have little to gain from an emergent State. Conflict has come to represent the norm, not a diversion from it. Few donors are willing to resume bilateral aid to Afghanistan when dialogue with a strong central government remains impossible. Afghanistan has become the classic 'weak state' (Duffield, 1994), suffering from systematic instability, and with declining strategic importance on the world stage.

Prince, merchant, and citizen: new roles in Afghanistan

Korten's model of functional complementarities between prince, merchant, and citizen does not resonate in the Afghan context. New divisions in Afghan society are based on political allegiance and wealth. CPEs are often characterised by the emergence of parallel economies beyond the control of the State. The new 'princes' in Afghanistan are the commanders and mullahs. For example, the economy of Jalalabad is now largely based on smuggling, opium production, and banditry, and it is the commanders with influence in the regional council who control and encourage such an economy.

As one enters Jalalabad, a long line of repainted vehicles for sale at the side of the road, mostly stolen in Peshawar, provide a stern reminder of the type of forces really in control of the area. (Cutts, 1993:14)

Civil society is intensely segmented and people's loyalties are directed towards family, clan, and lineage rather than community. Kinship loyalties have always been stronger than obligations towards the State. Dupree (1989: 249) describes the 'mud curtain' which villagers erect to protect themselves against the incursions of the State:

... once the modernisation teams leave, the villagers patch up the breaks in their mud curtain and revert to their old, group-reinforcing patterns.

The fragmentation of the resistance has led to a process of re-tribalisation; political allegiances have waned at the expense of a renewed ethnic awareness. The Tajiks, Hazaras, and Uzbeks, for example, have all found a new ethnic assertiveness as a result of the war. It is difficult to view such a chronically anarchic and divided society other than in Hobbesian terms. Villages have undergone the same process of fragmentation, with war sweeping away many of the traditional structures, and leaving an institutional vacuum, which has been subsequently filled by the military commanders.[2] There are few stable foundations from which to reconstruct.

The conflict has produced a combustible cocktail in which both the traditional and State constraints have been eroded, while the technological means to conduct war have become more sophisticated. NGOs are occupying the space left by the collapse of the State, and so wield great influence in the absence of effective government institutions.

The humanitarian response

The humanitarian response to the Afghan conflict reflects trends in global aid allocation. While development budgets are stagnating, there has been a marked increase in relief aid; and, since the 1980s, an enhanced role for NGOs. During the Cold War, when the UN was constrained by considerations of national sovereignty, NGOs attempted to supply humanitarian aid in contested areas (Duffield, op. cit.). NGOs are 'rushing in where soldiers and bureaucrats fear to tread' (Larmer, op. cit.), a phenomenon perpetuated by the sub-contracting of NGOs in areas where multilateral and bilateral agencies are unable or unwilling to get involved, such as controversial cross-border programmes.

With the 1979 Soviet occupation of Afghanistan, virtually all Western development programmes came to an end.[3] NGOs intervened through non-mandated cross-border programmes. Until 1988, NGOs were the principal means by which humanitarian relief and rehabilitation was provided to areas held by the Mujahideen. Initially, intervention was on a limited scale, involving fewer than 15 NGOs and between $5 and $10 million per year. By 1991, however, there were some 100 NGOs involved in such operations. In 1989,

total expenditure from the US government alone was $112 million (Nicholds and Borton, 1994).

The 1988 Geneva Accords included an agreement that, under UN auspices, the international community should undertake a substantial programme of relief and rehabilitation inside Afghanistan. The UN Secretary-General appointed a Coordinator for Humanitarian and Economic Assistance Programmes Relating to Afghanistan (UNOCA) to help to mobilise and coordinate resources. UNOCA (and many international donors) favoured strengthening the capacity of Afghan organisations to manage their own affairs, and 'Afghanisation' or 'de-foreignisation' entered the lexicon of Peshawar-based agencies.

UNOCA and other UN agencies thus encouraged the formation of Afghan NGOs (ANGOs), which were then sub-contracted for specific activities. The process is illustrated in the area of mine-clearance where, since the capacity of existing NGOs was limited, three were set up to cover different areas of Afghanistan (Nicholds and Borton, 1994).

By 1994, there were over 200 registered ANGOs (Barakat *et al.* 1994), often scathingly referred to as 'UN NGOs', reflecting a view that they were merely a fabrication of the donors. However, ANGOs have become major players in cross-border relief and rehabilitation work. In 1991, approximately 21 per cent of UNDP's $2 million budget was channelled via ANGOs, through 66 projects or contracts (Carter, 1991).

Typology of Afghan NGOs

The term 'Afghan NGOs' covers a range of organisations, many of which bear only a tenuous relationship to the family of NGOs. Carter (op. cit.), for example, argues that 'Afghan Implementing Agency' would be more accurate. Rahim (1991, cited in Nicholds and Borton, op. cit.) distinguishes four types:

1 Independent NGOs formed by non-affiliated professionals.

2 NGOs backed by local *shuras* (groups of elders) and commanders.

3 NGOs established by political parties, either individually or in coalition.

4 NGOs established by international organisations (UN or international NGOs).

A fifth, 'briefcase NGOs', might be added: these exist only in name, spawned in response to the easy availability of external funding. In reality, most ANGOs are hybrids: all, for example, have to develop links with parties, commanders, and local administrations, whether they are a UN 'spin-off' or a professional 'consultancy firm'. Most have developed from the top down, and they are now having to work backwards to find a community base of support (Carter, op. cit.).

Afghan NGOs: response to the conflict

Inevitably, such diversity has drawn varied assessments of ANGOs' roles and performance. Some claim that ANGOs could become the agents of transformation and reconstitute Afghan civil society from the bottom up. Critics argue that behind most ANGOs stands a foreign initiator and, therefore, a foreign definition of response to Afghan need. Pragmatists see a limited role for ANGOs, essentially as contracting mechanisms for the delivery of relief assistance.

CPEs have accelerated changes in the thinking and practice of humanitarian agencies, giving rise to the need for revised notions of change and causality (Roche, 1994). Relief and development are not discrete processes which unfold separately; the imperatives are similar in terms of addressing vulnerabilities and building capacities to enable communities to cope with change and survive future shocks (Anderson and Woodrow, 1989).

Some would argue that ANGOs may transcend the prevailing relief paradigm, and promote new forms of public action that build local capacities and foster peace. Rather than 'dancing with the prince', they constitute a countervailing force to the often arbitrary power of the prince.

Critics of the ANGO phenomenon argue that they were an opportunist response to a donor-led demand. Humanitarian agencies often respond to protracted crisis by '[replacing] well thought out, bottom-up participatory approaches, reintroducing the kind of top-down centrally driven crash programmes long ago discarded by the more thoughtful and experienced agencies' (ACORD, 1993:3). Baitenmann (1990) contends that most NGOs working cross-border were the conscious agents of political interests. In-field cooperation with combatants meant that NGOs made direct payments into the war economy. Cash-for-work projects, for example, were often re-directed to fund commanders' military activities. While NGOs may invoke the concept of neutral humanitarianism, 'dancing to the tune of the prince' has for them become an essential survival strategy.

A more pragmatic interpretation of ANGOs' role is that they are engaged in a holding operation. As Johnston and Clark (1982) note, 'when power confronts persuasion head-on, power wins' (p.13). By being non-confrontational, ANGOs may create some room for manoeuvre for themselves and for 'pro-citizen' groups within civil society. They may also have a role in protecting and nurturing future leaders, as they have in Latin America (Garilao, 1987).

Positive change in such an environment can occur only through a process of 'transformation through stealth' (Fowler, 1993). ANGOs have a 'Janus-headed role' (Edwards and Hulme, op. cit.), in which they claim to be apolitical, but have a core agenda of supporting democratisation and peace.

The relationship between ANGOs and the prince

The humanitarian response to CPEs is characterised by divergence between the rhetoric of neutrality and the reality of aid that is increasingly politicised. In Afghanistan, this response has become part of the political economy of violence. Cross-border operations were part of a political and ideological Cold War battle against the Soviets. Cross-border NGOs strengthened the base of the insurgency, their very presence legitimising the rebels (Baitenmann, op. cit.). It may be asked whether NGOs were indeed strengthening civil society, or rather attempting to shape it in ways that external actors considered desirable. Today, Afghanistan has lost its strategic value and is now what Duffield (op. cit.) describes as one of the 'weak states' on the margins of the global economy. Most of the Western players have made, or are making, a strategic withdrawal. A drip-feed of humanitarian assistance continues as a feature of the West's 'accommodation with violence' (Duffield, op. cit.), and the creation of ANGOs may have facilitated this withdrawal (Marsden, 1991).

Dancing with commanders and parties

ANGOs have two options in cross-border work: to cooperate with civilian authorities like *shuras*, or to develop ties with commanders. Initially, the latter was the only practicable option, since commanders constituted the real power-holders in any locality. In return for 'protection', commanders insisted on a share of donors' largesse. NGOs had a real impact on the local balance of power, by supporting some commanders in preference to others. They may thus have contributed to local conflicts and diminished social cohesion. Cash-for-food distributions in the early 1980s are an extreme example, where poorly monitored programmes are suspected of having provided Mujahideen commanders with funds for their military activities. Some donors were prepared to accept 'wastage levels' of up to *40 per cent* for their programmes in Afghanistan (Nicholds and Borton, op. cit.).

Channelling aid through commanders and parties has created precedents which NGOs find difficult to break. As military assistance declined, so humanitarian aid assumed importance as a source of patronage for commanders. Many NGOs have become an extension of the patron–client relationship between commanders and communities, and villagers clearly associate particular commanders with certain NGOs (Goodhand, 1992). The dilemma is that projects will not survive if they threaten the established power-holders; but unless they maintain a distance, they become part of the patronage system. Survival depends on understanding the local configurations of power, and success depends on the ability to draw on this authority without being co-opted by it. There is a fine line between survival as a means to an end, and survival as an end in itself.

The strategies adopted by ANGOs to remain operational in a turbulent environment are various. Some of them are considered below.

The human factor

The importance of creating space is illustrated in an ANGO director's comment that he spent 80 per cent of his time on political issues, 15 per cent on tribal matters, and only 5 per cent on the projects (Goodhand, op. cit.). ANGO managers have to be pragmatists, and they recognise that the support of commanders and parties is a prerequisite for survival. They must also have the Mujahideen credentials, party connections, and family background to build the necessary support and alliances, both inside and outside Afghanistan. Some ANGO managers may well emerge as future leaders of Afghan society. Working for an ANGO may, in retrospect, prove to be a more astute career path than that followed by the political party careerists.

Selective collaboration

ANGOs are playing a new game by old rules: an intricate balancing act of exploiting the 'economy of affection' of parties and commanders without being colonised by them. However, there is a danger of 'meeting villainy halfway'. The key to creating space is selective collaboration, rather than identifying with any one leader. It is a case of building strategic alliances with political and religious leaders, without losing one's room for manoeuvre.

Diversification

Some ANGOs have employed staff from various political backgrounds to guard against being partisan, and to maintain their range of options and contacts. Diversification is an essential strategy for survival; it is about trying to cover all your bases and to cope with uncertainty.

'Pointing the finger'

When under pressure, field staff are often able to deflect it by pointing the finger towards a distant authority outside the network of patronage — whether it is the head office, an expatriate adviser, or the donor. Donors and international staff can be valuable in absorbing such pressures on local NGOs, provided that there is a level of understanding and trust between the two parties.

Keeping a low profile

Keeping a low profile is about not making enemies. It may mean submerging one's identity and occasionally allowing the prince to take credit. A dual role is needed: the de-politicised public operation which emphasises humanitarianism, and the private operation which retains a core agenda of empowerment (Edwards and Hulme, op. cit.). Providing some bags of wheat to a commander, or employing some of his Mujahids, may be a necessary price for long-term gains.

Pragmatism and values: a Faustian pact?

When does the struggle for survival become an end in itself? At what stage does strategic co-operation become co-option? Many ANGOs have fallen into a kind of Faustian pact, in which 'eternal life' is brought at the price of their 'pro-citizen' soul. But all interventions represent an interaction between pragmatism and moral values, and the weighting given to each will vary with every decision. Manage-ment becomes the 'science of muddling through'. Responding to the demands of commanders involves a constant balancing of ends against means. Coherence comes through having a strong sense of values and a guiding philosophy. 'Dancing with the prince' may be a means to an ultimate end of peace and reconstruction.

The relationship between ANGOs and the citizen

UNOCA encouraged the development of ANGOs in the belief that they constituted the most effective mechanisms for delivering aid. Their understanding of the cultural and political dynamics of Afghan society, and their network of local contacts, enable them to get to the parts that international NGOs cannot reach. ANGOs have thus extended the reach of aid programmes to remote communities.

It has also been argued that ANGOs are not only more effective, but also more cost-efficient. A UNDP evaluation found that they had significantly lower costs than organisa-tions employing many expatriates (in Carter, op. cit.). Also, owing to the high turnover among expatriates, there was considerably more continuity within Afghan organisations than in international NGOs. Finally, ANGOs have provided on-the-job training, especially at the senior management level, which expatriate-run NGOs cannot provide. Many Afghans are now developing skills in manag-ing organisations and dealing with donors that will be essential in a future government (Carter, op. cit.).

Working behind the 'mud curtain'

ANGOs' principal advantage is that they were formed for Afghans by Afghans; as such, they have the political instincts and cultural awareness to act with sensitivity and caution in the complex web of Afghan society. Many Afghans have voiced a fear that external agencies undermine Afghan cultural values. ANGOs, however, can work quietly and carefully behind the 'mud curtain', and may thus also be producing an important resource: a cadre of 'organic intellectuals' with community-mobilisation skills.

Gender: constraints, openings, and missed opportunities

Conflict has brought new opportunities and new threats to NGOs seeking to address gender-related issues. While the disruption of the war years created an environment which challenges traditional gender roles, an upsurge in fundamentalism has tended further to restrict women's rights.

Most NGO projects aimed at women have worked with the relatively accessible refugees. It may never again be so easy to reach women from so many different parts of Afghanistan (Dupree, in Huld and Jansson, 1988). However, NGO attempts to work with women have tended to be rather superficial; handcraft and health projects, for example, that do not challenge existing power relations. ANGOs occupy an uneasy position; on the one hand, they are more vulnerable than international NGOs to conservative pressures from a patriarchal society. On the other, they are better able to work behind the 'mud curtain', where access to women is restricted to those with kinship and social ties. Currently, there are very few women in positions of reponsibility within ANGOs, and this will be slow to change. But ANGOs do at least have the understanding of social and cultural norms to recognise opportunities and take advantage of them.

While some commentators are optimistic about the possibilities for social change, the barriers are considerable.[4] Women's projects are often associated with the Communists' earlier attempts at 'social development'. One Pakistan-based ANGO director felt that if his group initiated activities that benefited women, he would be out of business in two weeks (Carter, op. cit.). If ANGOs confront the issue head-on, they may put their entire programme in jeopardy. Some ANGOs, after building up their credibility in a community, have incrementally introduced activities directed at women, though usually in traditional areas. Further success is likely to be slow and painstaking, requiring stealth as much as technical and managerial proficiency.

But however real the constraints, ANGOs have all too often avoided dealing with gender-based oppression on the grounds that it is 'too sensitive' or threatens local (patriarchal) culture. Thus opportunities have been missed to develop programmes that would directly benefit women in areas such as agriculture, fuel collection, and food production.

Reconstituting civil society?

The conflict has presented new opportunities in the sense that NGOs can work directly with communities, unencumbered by a government bureaucracy (Marsden, op. cit.). ANGOs may represent an important bridge between the people and emerging government structures. They can help to re-connect people with the State by communicating local needs to the government, and reducing the princes' monopoly over the flow of information. Optimistic observers would argue that ANGOs represent an alternative development path for Afghanistan: an alternative to the schizophrenic society produced by modernisation. Radical visions may, however, risk being associated with communism.

In rural Afghanistan, elders, religious leaders, and local *shuras* all function as stabilising points in a volatile environment. Most ANGOs have used these as the foundations for their projects, despite the danger of skirting round the issue of re-distributing power and resources; for instance, NGO interventions in the agricultural sector risk reinforcing a highly unequal structure. The issue is to strengthen indigenous capacity in a way consistent with humanitarian principles.

Rather than confront these issues directly, some ANGOs have tried an incrementalist approach. By focusing on productive activities, they have made a strategic response to practical needs. Many ANGOs, for example, have initiated *karez* (cleaning) programmes.[5] In the short term, this improves irrigation and thus food production; in the long term, such projects may develop into new forms of collective action. Some *karez* programmes have led to the revival of irrigation councils and to new village organisations coalescing around the ANGOs' projects. As Marsden (op. cit.) notes, there are few organisations in Afghan civil society above the grassroots level, and ANGOs may form an important nexus. Ultimately, collective action may become an empowering process which will meet the long-term strategic needs of vulnerable sectors — described earlier as 'transformation by stealth' (Fowler, op. cit.).

Demilitarising the mind

It is naive to imagine that ANGOs can be the catalysts for a grassroots peace movement in Afghanistan in the way that local NGOs have mobilised civil society in, for example, the Philippines and parts of Latin America. Any positive transformation will take place through small, incremental changes from the individual and community levels upwards. It is as much about demilitarising people's minds as about getting the princes together at the negotiating table. Although they could not explicitly refer to it as peace-building, ANGOs' work is contributing to a peace process within civil society. Several ANGO managers maintain that reconstruction and development will encourage Mujahids to lay down their guns, by offering them viable alternative livelihoods. Their projects embrace different tribal and ethnic groups which may also contribute to a peace process that can be built upwards by facilitating local cooperation (Marsden, op. cit.).

Questioning the comparative advantage of ANGOs

External organisations

'NGO lore' depicts ANGOs as an integral part of civil society, though in many respects the ANGO–community relationship mirrors the wider urban–rural divide. In a society where only 5–10 per cent of the population is literate, ANGO staff represent an educated elite, who entertain many of the biases and prejudices that education has imparted.

Although the leadership may be indigenous, the organisational model and response is not: it is that of Peshawar-based international NGOs. Consequently, ANGOs have reproduced and cultivated many of their models' intrinsic weaknesses. Like international NGOs, ANGOs tend to be based in Pakistan and are top-heavy, with more office staff than field staff.

The lack of long-term, flexible funding — including administrative costs — has trapped ANGOs in the 'project-by-project' system, thus reinforcing the image of ANGOs as service-providers, since they become contracting agencies for specific, time-bound projects, drawn up to someone else's agenda. ANGOs are not 'owned' by rural communities; they commonly 'belong' to donors, commanders, or Afghan technocrats. Thus they are accountable upwards to the donor or commander, but rarely downwards to the communities.

It is hard for ANGOs to insulate themselves from the ethnic, political, and religious pressures impinging upon them. Staff are under great pressure to benefit kith and kin, and some family-run ANGOs are susceptible to using assistance to improve the position and prestige of their family and clan (Carter, op. cit.). ANGOs have also been charged (like some international NGOs) with corruption. In Baitenmann's view (op. cit.), they were at least accessories to a relief programme that was plagued with corruption. And because of the clandestine nature of their work, cross-border NGOs were unavoidably drawn into a web of corruption, forced to pay bribes to Pakistani police or government officials, and protection levies for the right to travel within the country.

Most ANGOs were founded by charismatic individuals who have retained control over their organisation as it grows. This has inevitably placed these now powerful Afghan managers in an exposed position, accentuated by the political fluidity of Afghan society and the bitterness created by the conflict. Some ANGO personnel have been assassinated in recent years. Good political instincts are crucial for survival, both literally and figuratively. Such a situation militates against open and participatory management styles. The leader is unwilling to delegate authority because of the potential consequences of a 'bad' decision, so strategic planning tends to be subservient to crisis management. Centre–field relations become hierarchical, with field staff having little authority or status, and only the head-office senior managers allowed to see the whole picture.

Prisoners of a relief paradigm

There is some evidence that the general direction of change in NGO approaches has followed the pattern described by Korten: from the 'first generation' approach of relief and welfare, towards the 'second generation' stage of community development, and in some cases towards the 'third generation' stage of 'sustainable systems development' (Korten, op. cit.). Some cross-border NGOs are embracing development concepts related to community participation, monitoring and evaluation, participatory needs analysis, and so forth. However, they are influenced by a legacy of more than 15 years of relief operations. Most Afghan and international NGOs are still based in Pakistan, and find it difficult to break from their cross-border mode of operation.

Many NGOs have been active in Nangarhar Province in Eastern Afghanistan since the mid-1980s, because of its proximity to the Pakistan border. Free hand-outs were the norm and are now expected by local communities; relief has precluded, for the time being at least, an approach which places responsibility for development with local people. Critics would argue that the internal and external constraints already mentioned make ANGOs unlikely vehicles for transforming this paradigm. There is very little in their background to suggest that they can fulfil such a role. With their defining features — dependency on donors, staffed by a Kabul elite, hierarchical and centralised structures, susceptibility to penetration and colonisation — they appear singularly ill-equipped to transcend the prevailing pattern of relief. Even supposing this is part of their vision, the means are not consistent with the ends.

Going it alone

Over the years, NGOs working cross-border have demonstrated a remarkable inability to coordinate, or to avoid duplication. This 'lack of coordination and unified strategy amongst NGOs' was noted at a conference of ANGOs and donors (Barkat et al., op. cit.). Although coordination has since improved, it continues to be a problem for several reasons. Firstly, ANGOs are competing for a declining market-share of resources from donors. They may be responsive to demand, but it is a demand created by the donors, rather than by the beneficiaries. Projects become little more than pins on a map as evidence to meet the donors' criteria. Security and contacts, perhaps understandably, have been the primary factors in deciding where to work; long-term needs often appear almost incidental. Consequently, 150 NGOs are working in Jalalabad and less than a handful in the central province of Hazarajat. Coordination takes place in Pakistan, in isolation from relevant government departments in Afghanistan. A lack of coordination encourages duplication and undermines local initiative. For example, in 1994, the World Food Programme (WFP), by distributing food in Hazarajat, undermined the more participatory initiatives of local NGOs (Cutts, op. cit.).

A holding operation?

Claims that ANGOs can transcend the political pressures and their own internal limitations, to bring about a shift from relief assistance towards a more inclusive developmental approach, must still be treated with some scepticism. Afghanistan is not the dance floor for a confrontational 'pro-citizen' stance.

Most commonly, 'dancing with the prince' has involved co-option, or — at best — the creation of a little room for manoeuvre through compromise and selective collaboration.

ANGOs are not a panacea for the intractable problems of development in Afghanistan. They do, however, have a role to play in an environment where the State and civil society structures have been eroded. The key is to analyse the success stories — those ANGOs that have 'danced with the prince' and maintained their integrity — and develop strategies for replicating them.

Donors and their impact on the dance

The future direction of ANGOs will be determined largely by the policies of the donors and their intermediaries, the international NGOs. How can these identify, learn from, and 'scale up' the successes?

Firstly, their policies and practice should be based on an informed analysis of the nature of conflict and its relationship to development. This means recognising that conflict is a strategic issue, not to be ignored by the development planners.

Secondly, a more flexible and long-term response is required. In Afghanistan, funding requests were often turned down on the basis that they were 'too developmental'; donors' thinking and institutional arrangements are based on linear notions of the 'relief to development continuum'. Experience in Afghanistan exposed the lack of institutional frameworks within which to provide assistance for *transitional* activities which are neither 'relief' or 'development'.

Thirdly, a more informed political analysis is vital. In Afghanistan, donors must make difficult choices about which princes or which citizens to support. What are the political implications of policies which strengthen provincial structures rather than central government, or ANGOs rather than community organisations? It needs to be explicitly acknowledged that ANGOs do have a political role, in that they can affect and are affected by the dynamics of the conflict. It is naive to regard them purely as service-delivery mechanisms.

Towards a new form of engagement

There are tensions in trying to achieve multiple objectives in supporting NGOs. For example, funding ANGOs for delivering relief — to meet the objectives of the donors — has often been to the detriment of longer-term aims of capacity-building. Ways are needed to broaden the relationship beyond that of being simply partners in aid delivery. Duffield (op. cit.) argues that engagement should be linked to a 'new ethics': showing solidarity, rather than keeping a distance from the fray and paying lip-service to neutrality.

Fine words, but what do they mean in practice? A starting point must be a broader and more flexible relationship between donors and ANGOs: breaking out of the 'project syndrome' (where projects and development are assumed to be synonymous), and making a long-term and open-ended commitment to selected ANGOs. Projects in Afghanistan are often risky and involve slow and careful work which cannot be melded into 'projectised chunks'. This means moving from the 'culture of concrete results'. However, although capacity-building is a fashionable term, it is not always clear what it actually means. In Afghanistan, it often translates into building the capacity of ANGOs to implement their donors' agendas. However capacity-building should not be limited to 'skilling up' organisations, or providing a technical fix. It implies a wider dialogue, based on shared values and ethics. Some donors and NGOs have now started to work in this way, to formulate working principles for peace-building and reconstruction in Afghanistan (Barakat *et al.*, op. cit.).

In general, ANGOs have had to dance to the tunes of both the donor and the prince. These roles need to be reversed in order to make a reality of the civil-society rhetoric. A starting point might be to introduce mechanisms that empower organisations *within* civil society, whether these be NGOs or community groups, to help to set the agenda and so call the tune.

Notes

1 According to the UNDP 1994 *Human Development Report*, in 1993 42 countries experienced 52 major conflicts and another 37 countries experienced political violence. Only three of the 82 conflicts between 1989 and 1992 were between States. In 1993–4 alone, there were 4 million deaths as a result of ethno-political wars, mostly of civilians. Without an effective international ombudsman and with the thriving international arms trade, conflict is bound to continue.

2 Many NGOs latched on to the concept of *shuras* (councils of elders), believing them to be stable, community-based organisations which could be building blocks in the reconstruction process. However, this is to misunderstand the character and role of *shuras*, which are loose consultative bodies, brought together on an *ad hoc* basis to discuss particular issues or resolve conflicts (Marsden, 1991).

3 Neither the UN nor the International Committee of the Red Cross (ICRC) could work cross-border; the UN because of its mandate to work with recognised governments, and ICRC because it could not secure the consent of all parties to the conflict.

4 The emergence of the Taleban (a movement of religious students) from late 1994 has further narrowed the scope for agencies involved in women's programmes. The Taleban now control much of the country and insist that women and girls remain within the confines of their compounds.

5 *Karezes* are traditional underground irrigation systems.

References

ACORD (1993) Annual Report, 1993
Anderson, M B and P J Woodrow (1989), *Rising from the Ashes: Development Strategies in Times of Disaster*, Boulder/Paris: Westview/UNESCO
Baitenmann, H (1990) 'NGOs and the Afghan war: the politicisation of humanitarian aid', *Third World Quarterly*, Vol. 12 no. 1
Barakat, S, M Ehsan, and A Strand (1994) *NGOs and Peace-Building in Afghanistan: Workshop Report*, University of York, England
Carter, L with A Eichfield (1991) 'Afghan Non-Governmental Organisations and Their Role in the Rehabilitation of Afghanistan', unpublished report for International Rescue Committee, Peshawar, Pakistan
Clark, J (1991) *Democratising Development: the Role of Voluntary Organisations*, London: Earthscan
Cutts, M (1993) 'Report on SCF Visit to the North Western, Central and Eastern Regions of Afghanistan', unpublished report, London: The Save the Children Fund
Duffield, M (1994) 'Complex emergencies and the crisis of developmentalism', *IDS Bulletin: Linking Relief and Development*, vol 25, no 3
Dupree, L (1989) *Afghanistan*, New Jersey: Princetown University Press
Edwards, M and D Hulme (1995) 'NGOs and development; performance and accountability in the "New World Order"' in Edwards and Hulme (eds) (1995) *Non-Governmental Organisations — Performance and Accountability: Beyond the Magic Bullet*, London: Earthscan with The Save the Children Fund
Fowler, A (1993) 'NGOs as agents of democratisation: an African perspective', *Journal of International Development*, vol 5 no 3
Garilao, E (1987) 'Indigenous NGOs as strategic institutions: managing the relationship with government and resource agencies', *World Development*, Vol. 15, Supplement, pp. 113-120
Goodhand, J (1992) 'Report of the Rural Assistance Programme Cross Border Training Programme', unpublished report, International Rescue Committee, Peshawar, Pakistan

Huld, B and E Jansson (1988) *The Tragedy of Afghanistan: The Social, Cultural and Political Impact of the Soviet Invasion*, London: Croom Helm

Johnston B and M Clark (1982) *Redesigning Rural Development: A Strategic Perspective*, London: Johns Hopkins Press

Korten, D C (1990) *Getting to the 21st Century: Voluntary Action and the Global Agenda*, London: Routledge

Larmer, B (1994) 'The new colonialism', *Newsweek*, 1 August 1994

Macrae, J and A Zwi (1992) 'Food as an instrument of war in contemporary African Famines', *Journal of Disaster Studies*, Vol. 16 no. 4

Marsden, P (1991) *Afghanisation*, London: British Agencies Afghan Group

Nicholds, N and J. Borton (1994) *The Changing Role of NGOs in the Provision of Relief and Rehabilitation Assistance: Case Study 1 — Afghanistan/Pakistan*, ODI Working Paper 74, London: Overseas Development Institute

Roche, C (1994) 'Operationality in turbulence: the need for change', *Development in Practice*, Vol. 4, no. 3

Roy, O (1989) 'Afghanistan: back to tribalism or on to Lebanon?', *Third World Quarterly*, Vol. 11, no. 4

Rupesinghe, K (1994) *Advancing Preventative Diplomacy in a Post-Cold War Era: Suggested Roles for Governments and NGOs*, ODI Relief and Rehabilitation Network, Network Paper 5, September, 1994, London: Overseas Development Institute

Slim, H (1994) 'The continuing metamorphosis of the humanitarian professional: some new colours for an endangered chameleon', *Disasters*

The authors

Jonathan Goodhand worked for the International Rescue Committee in Afghanistan (1987-90) and as distribution coordinator for Save the Children Fund in Sri Lanka (1992–94), before taking up his current post as Central Asia Programme Manager at INTRAC. **Peter Chamberlain** worked for the Austrian Relief Committee in Pakistan (1989-93) and since 1995 has been Oxfam's emergency programme coordinator based in Goma, Zaire.

This article first appeared in *Development in Practice*, Volume 6, Number 3, in 1996.

The role of Salvadorean NGOs in post-war reconstruction

Francisco Alvarez Solís and Pauline Martin

Introduction

On 16 January 1992, the Salvadorean Government and the leadership of the Farabundo Martí Liberation Front (FMLN) signed a Peace Agreement which 'would put a definitive end to the armed conflict'.[1] Eleven years of civil war and over a year of intense negotiation, mediated by the United Nations Secretary-General, ended in a formal ceremony in Mexico City. The Peace Accords set the political and military framework for the reduction of the Armed Forces, the demobilisation of FMLN combatants, and the legalisation of the insurgents as a political force inside El Salvador. The Agreement also includes 'a minimum platform of commitments to facilitate development (social and economic) for the benefit of all sectors of the population' (PA, 42).

The reconstruction of El Salvador may have passed to the top of the Central American agenda. However, it is the terms on which it is undertaken which will determine the possibilities of a lasting peace. These, in turn, will depend upon the capacity of national and international policy makers to address the social and economic roots of conflict and crisis in El Salvador.

The war, economic crisis, and natural disasters during the 1980s have between them caused huge losses of human life and extensive destruction of the national infrastructure and natural resources. An enormous price has been paid in terms of social disintegration: an estimated total of between 1.17 and 1.65 million Salvadoreans have been forced to leave their homes — between a quarter and a third of the population. For those who stayed in the country, there has been increased impoverishment. These factors, together with the deterioration and destruction of basic services and damage to production, are some of the main problems which will have to be addressed in reconstruction strategies.[2]

The Salvadorean Government puts total losses for the decade at US$ 1,579 million, and costs of repairs and replacements at US$1,627 million.[3] The latter figure is equivalent to 44 per cent of the economic and military aid provided by the United States government from 1979 to 1990, which reached a total of US$3,732 million.[4] The amount is also equivalent to only 6 per cent less than the capital flight from 1980 to 1988, which is estimated at US$1,732 million.[5] In operational terms, the amount needed is equivalent to 2.6 times the 1991 national budget.

Material reconstruction and the process of repairing El Salvador's social and cultural fabric will require the mobilisation of human, institutional, and financial resources on a massive scale, both nationally and internationally — this at a time when there are demands for international aid from other parts of the world, perhaps considered more strategic than Central America in terms of political stability and trading potential.

Against this background, this article sets out to explore the various components of reconstruction — what is needed and how this might be achieved. In this context, it will contrast the declared aims of the Government's National Reconstruction Plan (NRP) with the experience in social development accumulated by NGOs and social organisations during the war years. In particular, it will point to the need for national and local reconstruction strategies to incorporate the active participation of communities, their own representative structures, and the NGOs which have worked with them, if they are to ensure a lasting peace in El Salvador.

The experience and potential of NGOs

During the period 1952 to 1979, there were only 22 NGOs registered in El Salvador. From 1980 to 1991, the number increased more than threefold to 74.[6] The proliferation of NGOs was an attempt by different sectors of Salvadorean society to respond during the 1980s to the problems created by war, social and economic crisis, and natural disasters.[7] The presence of NGOs in the polarised context of civil war established a kind of mediation between the unsatisfied needs of the population and the social and economic policies of successive governments. However, NGOs have often been assumed to have political sympathies, or indeed have aligned themselves with one of the parties in the conflict.

González (1991) gives a number of explanations for the increased numbers of NGOs in the 1980s. Among them, he mentions:

- economic support from the US Government;
- the reform policies of the Salvadorean Government;
- widespread deterioration in living conditions;
- counter-insurgency and military 'civic action' programmes;
- the social cost of the war and the humanitarian response;
- international NGO funding.

He defines NGOs as falling into five main categories, according to how they originated or who set them up. These are:

- the churches (Catholic and Protestant), some of which have mediated between the Government and the FMLN;
- donor governments or international NGOs;
- political parties;
- communities of displaced people (a variation of grassroots organisations);
- groups sponsored by the Salvadorean Government, but called NGOs.

In response to war and widespread political violence throughout Central America, the people most affected developed new forms of social organisation for self-defence and survival during the 1980s. Many of these defined themselves as popular organisations, and as part of a popular movement with a common platform for social and economic change. As traditional political-party structures lost credibility in much of civil society, so the popular organisations became the main channel of participation for large numbers of people who were otherwise marginalised. In El Salvador in particular, the popular organisations became vital channels of humanitarian aid, especially to displaced people and to refugees returning to the country.

Thus many of the 1980s generation of NGOs are essentially the institutional expression of sectors of the urban and rural poor who organised to defend themselves from violence and repression. A wealth of experience has been accumulated in humanitarian assistance, non-formal education, and community-based economic and social development, particularly in areas and communities most seriously affected by the war.

Salvadorean NGOs developed considerable administrative experience and operational capacity in the process. They had support in this from international agencies, as well as through bilateral and multilateral aid. This has been extremely important in the development of the Salvadorean NGO sector, irrespective of the political persuasion of donors or recipients.

The existence of such NGOs and social organisations is a concrete manifestation of the energy, creativity, and organisational and negotiating capacity developed by poor people, simply in order to survive.

The inefficiency of the State, the diversion of resources to military spending, and the application of structural adjustment measures — leading to privatisation of public services — vastly increased social need. At the same time, this meant an expansion in the opportunities for NGOs to take on a role in social development. Their effectiveness in this work can be measured by the trust they have gained from the beneficiary population, and by the extent to which project and programme work has been able to address the needs of the poorest sectors.

There are negative trends too. The NGO 'boom' also brought competition, duplication, lack of planning, poor coordination, and a lack of self-critical evaluation. Most of their structures, priorities, and programmes were established and implemented in a context of emergency. Today, NGOs are in a process of reassessing their roles. They are also analysing their relationships with their beneficiaries or constituencies, with each other, the State, their current donors, and potential funders who may be seeking ways of channelling resources on a larger scale.

NGOs with a strong background in working with poor communities and displaced people during the war years are well placed to play an important function in national reconstruction. To do so, however, the nature and quality of the work they carried out must be recognised by the Salvadorean government, as well as by international donors. In the short term, such NGOs need to define common strategies in relation to two crucial factors: first, the Peace Agreement and the Government's National Reconstruction Plan (NRP) for social and economic recovery; and second, USAID and the multilateral agencies, in particular the World Bank, Inter-American Development Bank (IDB), and United Nations Development Programme (UNDP).

The peace agreements and the National Reconstruction Plan

One of the Agreements was that the Salvadorean government would present a National Reconstruction Plan (NRP) to the FMLN and to different sectors of society, including the NGOs, for discussion, 'with the intention that recommendations and suggestions would be taken into account' and 'that the Plan would reflect a common will in the country' (PA, 52).

The Peace Agreement defines three principal objectives within the NRP: firstly, the integration and development of areas affected by the conflict; secondly, attention to the immediate needs of those most affected by the conflict and to the needs of ex-combatants of both sides; and thirdly, rebuilding of damaged infrastructure.

The government, with the support of the UNDP, agreed to facilitate the channelling of international aid by setting up a National Reconstruction Fund (PA, 53). The UNDP also has a key role to play in mobilising international aid, planning projects, providing technical assistance, and ensuring compatibility between governmental and non-governmental plans at local and regional level (PA, 53). In the specific case of NGOs, the government would aim to 'approve legal and institutional facilities for external private aid destined for communities, social organisations and NGOs provided it could be established that they were developing or wished to develop integrated development projects' (PA, 50).

The National Reconstruction Plan[8] underlines the Government's stated intention to promote broad-based participation in national reconstruction and to forge social consensus around it. To bring about such participation, the NRP identifies specific roles and functions for NGOs and communities. For example, both State institutions and NGOs may be contracted by local mayors for developing projects which have been approved as priority through local public assemblies (*cabildeos abiertos*). State entities, including the Secretariat for National Reconstruction (SRN) which answers directly to the President, may also contract the services of NGOs or community organisations to carry out projects. However, NGOs and community organisations will be allowed to develop their own projects and programmes only after approval by the SRN.

In the light of such prescriptions for NGO and community participation in the NRP, certain conclusions can be drawn:

1 The government sees the NGOs as private entities to be contracted for defined services. Their participation is limited to the implementation of specific programmes or projects.

2 There is no recognition of those organisations who represent the beneficiary communities.

3 Local government is accorded very significant levels of responsibility in the coordination, administration, and implementation of programmes at both local and regional levels.

4 The participation of NGOs and social organisations in the Secretariat for National Reconstruction is not contemplated: in fact, the SNR is established as a top-down structure to impose policy.

The State apparently seeks to be the protagonist in national reconstruction. Yet there seems to be little real recognition that popular organisations and NGOs have eleven years' experience in working precisely in the areas of the country and with those social sectors which were abandoned by the State, both before and during the war years.

An additional difficulty concerns the distribution of the budget. The third draft of the Plan, published in February 1992, provides two budgets. The first puts a figure of US$1,627 million on reconstruction costs, of which 3 per cent would be allocated to health, education and housing, 4 per cent to agriculture, and 93 per cent to infrastructure. However, the budget by sector and projects

assumes a total figure of only US$1,304 million, of which 30 per cent would be allocated to the social sector and human capital, 31 per cent to infrastructure, 19 per cent to production, 6 per cent to environment, 12 per cent to democracy programmes, and 2 per cent to technical assistance.

The differences in total budgets and the allocations outlined are large, and it is apparent that final budgets are yet to be approved.

USAID and the multilateral agencies

The reconstruction scenario would be incomplete without a brief analysis of the roles of both USAID and the multilateral agencies (mentioned above) within it.

USAID was the main source of foreign funding to the Salvadorean government during the 1980s. In fact, El Salvador became the third major recipient of US foreign aid in the world, with only Israel and Egypt receiving higher amounts. USAID is now a key player in the design of the National Reconstruction Plan, within the context of its overall strategy for Latin America. In its 'Economic Assistance Strategy for Central America: 1991 to 2000', USAID announced a change in its approach to the region:

There is an unprecedented opportunity over the next decade to achieve the political stability, economic prosperity and social justice that have for so long eluded the people of Central America.

These objectives are set in the broader framework of the Bush Administration's vision for Latin America, as presented in two recent policy statements. The 'Enterprise of the Americas Initiative' (EAI) is intended for all of Latin America, and focuses on free trade, investment, and debt reduction. It links democracy, trade, and investment as the basis of sustainable economic growth. The policy was summarised by President Bush as 'free governments and free markets'. The second policy statement, 'The Partnership for Democracy and Development in Central America', creates a forum for fostering international support for regional development in Central America; and aims to promote a coordinated approach to bilateral and multilateral aid, placing particular emphasis on strengthening democratic institutions.

Thus, USAID is explicitly aiming to further US strategic interests in Central America. It plans to support the positive trends it sees by consolidating democratic societies, and by promoting sustainable economic growth and regional cooperation. At the same time, with diminished resources, it is looking to encourage other donors to help to foot the bill.

Throughout Latin America, USAID also envisages an increased role for NGOs in the context of further cuts in State spending and public services and the transfer of productive activity and services to the private sector. Municipal governments, the private sector, and NGOs are seen as playing a more active part, especially in the provision of social services. In general, USAID aims to involve the NGO sector in the following ways:

• *Democracy programmes to improve civil participation*: funds will be channelled through NGOs for civic education, including through the schools, and strengthening of judicial systems.

• *Welfare and social services*: funds for health care, family planning, nutrition for the poor, and increased efficiency in delivery systems would be handled by NGOs. Proposals include the use of debt-swap arrangements for family-planning services to be delivered through the NGOs.

• *Environment*: local and national NGOs will be engaged to work on environmental concerns.

• *Sustainable development*: USAID will help NGOs and governments to develop policies, laws, and programmes for sustainable agriculture, especially land use.

However, the Salvadorean counterparts for USAID do not fall within the NGO sector. Instead, USAID works largely through the National Commission for the Restoration of Areas (CONARA), which was involved in civic action programmes in conflict areas as part of counter-insurgency strategies. The multilateral agencies — World Bank, IDB, and UNDP — together with USAID, are assisting the Cristiani Government in the design of its economic and social policies. These include the establishment of the Salvadorean Social Investment Fund (Fondo de Inversion Social Salvadorena — FISS). This is intended to administer social compensation programmes, as a means of cushioning the worst effects of structural adjustment programmes on the poorest, similar to the programmes already being operated in Costa Rica, Guatemala, Honduras, and Nicaragua.

A number of bilateral donors, especially Scandinavian and European Community governments, are making their aid conditional on greater involvement of NGOs. However, the Salvadorean government is demonstrating caution. One observer describes attempts to incorporate NGOs in the FISS:

The limited effort to create a framework to incorporate NGOs into the FISS reflects government policy to work only with NGOs with proven links to business groups, and the IDB's relative inexperience of welfare-orientated NGOs. The IDB's cautious and unimaginative hands-on approach has not pushed government to deal with an NGO sector [which] government considers subversive.[9]

The overall intentions of USAID for Central America are compatible with the aims of the National Reconstruction Plan in El Salvador. They each promote the discourse of consensus-building, social participation, and democracy. But the rhetoric has yet to translate into a development practice which will ensure that the stated aims of 'political stability, economic prosperity and social justice' are able to be met.

The response of local NGOs

Five major Salvadorean NGO networks were active during the war in humanitarian relief and social development with refugees, displaced people, and repatriated communities throughout the entire country. Joining their efforts in a loose coalition body, the Concertación Nacional,[10] they see themselves as

working towards — and contributing to the formulation of — a single national plan for reconstruction. Such a 'Civil Society Reconstruction Plan' would represent planning input, as well as implementation activities by a wide range of governmental and non-governmental entities.[11]

These NGOs argue the need for a National Reconstruction Plan whose success will depend upon comprehensive participation and consensus in its design as well as its implementation. Such a Plan would require a new vision of social and economic development and a modification of the 'emergency and compensation' approach which has deepened the poverty of the poorest.

The Plan should legitimise and institutionalise the participation of civil society in its various expressions, especially participation of the new socio-economic actors that arose during the war, as well as of those from the popular movement and its institutional representatives ... The Plan should become an arena for consensus building to advance the construction of a new model of the prosperous, just and democratic society to which we aspire for El Salvador.[12]

These NGOs have been invited by the government to take part in discussions of the National Reconstruction Plan. However, they make major criticisms of the NRP, observing that it is based on out-dated concepts of development which have failed in the past in Latin America and which aim to stimulate economic growth with little attention to social development or to environmental protection.

They are concerned that it is not the result of a process of building a broad-based social consensus, and that the Salvadorean government plans to control implementation in a way which does not permit the direct participation of representative social organisations in decision-making.

The Plan is also criticised because it creates beneficiaries, rather than active participants in the process of reconstruction, ignoring local-level organisational structures and their years of experience in self-development.

The coverage of the Plan is seen to be inadequate. It addresses a target population of 826,117 people in 99 municipalities; yet El Salvador has a population of over 5 million in 262 municipalities.[13] Moreover, it concentrates exclusively on the rural population directly affected by the conflict, and ignores the large and expanding urban population living in extreme poverty.

Finally, critics argue that the government lacks the social base to implement the proposed programmes, and the resources to implement them. The lack of consensus in the formulation of the Plan is likely to dissuade the international community from funding it.

Prospects for post-war reconstruction

Presidential elections are scheduled for 1994, and the FMLN is expected to participate as a political organisation. Demands for rapid responses from all levels of society will exert pressure on the government; and reconstruction plans will be expected to provide the basis for answers. One of the key problems for Cristiani's government is how to bring people together in the cause of national reconstruction. The NRP states that its success depends on political viability and 'a minimum consensus between the country's social and political forces; the active participation of the population which will benefit from the projects ...' (NRP, 16).

In our view, one of the principal issues which will cause tension between the government and the popular sectors is the economic framework in which the government has defined the NRP. The Plan states that 'it must be consistent with the global aims of the macro-economic programme and complementary to the Government's investment plan' (NRP, 15). In other words, the Plan has to be consistent with structural adjustment policies. To date, the effects of these policies in El Salvador have been similar to the results of their application throughout Latin America and the Caribbean.

Yet, by stating that the Reconstruction Plan is a political as well as an economic instrument, the government makes plain its wish to restore the legitimacy of the State by gaining the confidence of the people: '[The government possesses] the legitimacy to carry through the political projections on which it based its electoral campaign ... the NRP constitutes a political project' (NRP, 13). Similarly, the local assemblies (*cabildeos abiertos*) are envisaged as a mechanism for meeting two objectives: 'strengthening the legitimacy of the State and democratising decision-making on programmes and projects for the communities' (NRP, 12).

The economic orientation of the Plan, its limited institutional and administrative structure, and the intention of the government to use it as a political instrument together suggest that many social and popular organisations, NGOs, political parties, and churches will opt to redefine their participation. Other groups, such as NGOs which work with government programmes or demobilised members of the armed forces, may provide a limited social base of support. However, a National Reconstruction Plan cannot forge the social consensus and active support considered essential for its success if it becomes simply the political project of the Government or of one political party.

Lessons from Nicaragua

The Salvadorean NGO community has already made important advances in coordinating its strategies to highlight deficiencies in existing government plans; and to put forward alternatives based upon NGOs' own considerable experience in providing humanitarian assistance, and promoting social and economic development in the context of civil war.

The experience of NGO work in Nicaragua under the Sandinista government (1979-90) is salutary and relevant. It points to certain risks which their Salvadorean colleagues may need to consider — and which may have broader relevance to post-war reconstruction programmes elsewhere in the world.[14] From the perspective of the national NGOs, there are three main areas of potential difficulty:

- Competition between NGOs for funds, influence and power, especially in the case of those working in the same geographical area or sector.
- Competition between NGOs and popular organisations, all seeking to be the counterparts of donor agencies.
- A tendency to 'package and sell' projects which the NGOs considered to be attractive to the donors — resulting in many projects which responded more to supply from the North than to a demand from the South based on a clear strategy for sustainable alternatives in development.

For the international donor NGOs, other problems also arise. There may be tensions between NGOs competing for the same counterpart organisations or projects; and competition between international NGOs from the same country for access to their own government's aid budget, or to funds raised from the general public. There may in addition be differences of opinion between confessional and secular agencies and between church-linked agencies. And, cutting across all of these tensions, there may be conflicting theoretical and methodological approaches to humanitarian aid and social development.

There are also difficulties which affect relations between national NGOs and international donor agencies. These tend to arise when there is not sufficient clarity about the specific role of each. It may be very much harder to define such roles during a period of transition from one context to another — in the case of Nicaragua, from a revolutionary to a conservative government committed to neo-liberal policies. In a new setting, old methodologies may no longer be the most appropriate.

Finally, for all autonomous NGOs, there is the ever-present risk of co-option by the State or by political parties.

Hopes and fears: some conclusions

At the time of writing, the people of El Salvador are living through a complex transition from eleven years of war towards the promise and the expectation of peace. The Peace Agreement provides a basic political framework for ending the conflict and rebuilding the country. But national concilia-tion in El Salvador cannot be decreed, and is certainly not created by signatures on documents in Mexico.

The National Reconstruction Plan of the Salvadorean government does not in our view inspire much hope that it has the will or the ability to go beyond party-political interests to build a broad-based consensus around rebuilding the country. The Plan's restriction to existing economic policies, and the exclusion of key social sectors from real participation in planning and decision-making, suggest increased social polarisation. And communities in areas of conflict, to which the Plan gives priority, have demonstrated in the past their capacity to block programmes which have attempted to assimilate them.

NGOs, social and popular organisations, and other sectors are drawing up their own proposals for national reconstruction and will offer them to the international community as an alternative plan. This approach draws on the experience of the International Conference for Central American Refugees (*Conferencia Internacional para los Refugiados Centro-americanos — CIREFCA*), which has been a three-year process involving donors, Central American governments, and national and international NGOs. The process itself provides a valuable experience and example of consultation and joint planning between governments and NGOs, as a result of which, shared positions and strategies have been reached.[15]

At the heart of the debate lies the urgent need for more creative thinking on how to design strategies for more equitable development and sustainable growth which address the roots of conflict and crisis in El Salvador. The Peace Agreement offers many opportunities to begin to build a stable and democratic society; it also contains the risk that the cycle of poverty, violence, and repression will not be broken.

Notes

1   Gobierno de El Salvador y Frente Farabundo Marti de Liberacion Nacional (January 1992). (Succeeding references to this document will refer to Peace Agree-ment (PA), with the page number of the document.)

2   The United Nations Economic Commiss-ion for Latin America and the Caribbean (CEPAL) reported in December 1990 the following consequences of a decade of war and economic crisis: 70,000 people killed (combatants and civilians); 500,000 people displaced inside the country (10 per cent of the total population); 447 schools closed, due to partial or total destruction, or to poor security; a 20 per cent drop in GNP per capita; an estimated 68 per cent of the population living below the poverty line (CEPAL, December 1990).

3   These figures do not include the material damages caused to the rural population, especially refugees and displaced people.

4   Roberto Codas F. and Francisco Alvarez S., September 1990, page 35.

5   Roberto Codas F., July 1990, page 30.

6   Victor González, August 1991.

7   An earthquake in 1986, drought and floods each year since 1987.

8   Ministry of Planning and Coordination of

Economic and Social Development, Executive Summary, February 1992. This is the third draft of the Plan. Each version has carried different budgetary information.

9   Peter Sollis, 1991.

10 The five are ASDI (Asociación Salvadoreña de Desarrollo Integral), CORDES (Fundación para la Cooperación con Pobladores y Desplazados Salvadoreños), FASTRAS (Fundación para la Autogestión y Solidaridad de los Trabajadores Salvadoreños), FUNSALPRODESE (Fundación Salvadoreña para la Promoción del Desarrollo Social y Economico), and REDES (Fundacion Salvadoreña para la Reconstrucción y Desarrollo).

11 Report on the Concertación Nacional visit to Washington DC, January 1992, prepared by the Unitarian Universalist Service Committee.

12 Salvadorean NGO Association, 'Comments on Reconstruction: How its Work with Repatriates and the Displaced Shapes the views of Concertación Nacional', Washington, January 1992.

13 These figures are taken from the second draft of the National Reconstruction Plan, published in September 1991. The third draft of February 1992 mentions 800,000 people in 106 municipalities mainly in the north of the country. According to the FMLN, there is a total of 200 municipalities in El Salvador.

14 These are reflections of a consultant who has worked in Nicaragua for a decade, for an internal coordination meeting of NGOs. The document is for restricted circulation, and the authors of this article are not authorised to quote from it. However, they will make reference to a number of points, given their relevance for El Salvador.

15 The next CIREFCA conference was due to take place in San Salvador in April 1992. Following months of work to improve NGO participation in national planning of projects for refugees and displaced people, the government and NGOs were due to present a joint position to the conference.

The attitude of several major donors has been very important in stressing the importance of the NGO input; they have in some cases made their aid conditional on such participation.

References

Agency for International Development (January 1991), 'Economic Assistance Strategy for Central America: 1991-2000', Washington DC.

CEPAL (December 1990), 'El Salvador: El Estado de la Pobreza y Lineamientos de Política para Afrontarla'.

Codas F., Roberto (September 1990), 'El perfil externo del sistema socioeconómico salvadoreño', San Salvador: PREIS.

Codas F., Roberto, and Francisco Alvarez S. (1990), 'La asistencia de Estados Unidos a El Salvador en los ochenta; una revisión preliminar', San Salvador: PREIS.

Concertación Nacional de El Salvador (July 1992), 'Salvadoran NGO Association Comments on National Reconstruction', Washington DC: Unitarian Universalist Service Committee.

Cordes, Diaconia et al., 'CIREFCA: el proceso de concertación entre las ONG's y el Gobierno de El Salvador'.

Frente Farabundo Marti Para La Liberacion Nacional (February 1992), 'Propuesta a la Nación; Plan de reconstrucción para el desarrollo de la nueva sociedad salvadoreña; versión preliminar', San Salvador.

Gobierno de El Salvador (September 1991), 'Plan de Recuperación Económica y Social Nacional (PRESN), versión preliminar', Vol. 1, San Salvador.

Gobierno de El Salvador (February 1992), 'Plan de Reconstrucción Nacional de El Salvador', Resumen Ejecutivo, San Salvador.

Gobierno de El Salvador y Frente Farabundo Martí Para La Liberación Nacional (January 1992), 'Acuerdo de paz', Mexico.

González, Victor (August 1991), 'Las

Organizaciónes No Gubernamentales —
ONGs: Una nueva expresión de la Sociedad
Civil Salvadoreña', San Salvador.
Sollis, Peter (1991), 'Poverty Alleviation in El
Salvador: An Appraisal of the Christiani Gov-
ernment's Social Programme' (unpublished).

The authors

Francisco Alvarez Solìs is a Salvadorean
sociologist at present studying in Mexico. He
has worked on development-related research
projects at the Universidad Centroamericana
(UCA) and EDC-Alternatives for Development in San Salvador. Until 1990 he was based
at PREIS, a Salvadorean NGO which conducts
and publishes socio-economic research. He has
written a thesis on the experience of repatriation of refugees to El Salvador, and the return of
internally displaced people to their homes.

Pauline Martin is Regional Manager for
Oxfam (UK and Ireland), responsible for
Mexico, Central America, and the Caribbean.
She has worked in Latin America for fourteen
years. In the UK, she has published research on
education in Chile. Following a year based in a
Salvadorean NGO, she has also published
papers in El Salvador on international
cooperation in Central America.

This article was first published in
Development in Practice Volume 2, Number 2
(1992). Since it was written, the peace process
in El Salvador has taken many directions, some
of which point to the inadequacies of the terms
of the Peace Accords. For further information,
refer to the Washington Office on Latin
America, which publishes authoritative briefings on the region.

Children of war in the Philippines

Hàns Buwalda

Introduction

The problems of children in war-time are generally not dealt with in much of the literature on development. However, some organisations, particularly in countries where political armed conflict rages, are increasingly realising that children are often victimised in the process; and that this has important ramifications, not only for the children as individuals but also for social development more generally. In various countries, there are groups in the process of setting up programmes to help children deal with the trauma resulting from war. But they suffer from a lack of expertise.

This article[1] looks at the children of war in the Philippines. It is based on my experiences as a Western-trained therapist working with those involved in development issues; and specifically with children suffering from, or potentially facing, war-related traumatisation. It provides an account of combining a Western therapeutic approach with an indigenous programme of therapy for young war victims, as developed by the Children's Rehabilitation Center in Davao City.[2] This may provide a way of dealing with the larger social problems among children growing up with violence.

War-related trauma in children

We all structure our own environment: all human beings try to find a basic logic, or to establish an explanation connecting the things we perceive, know, and feel into a more or less comprehensible unity. War disrupts this process, especially for children who are caught up in it.

Children of war often show symptoms of severe psychological trauma: sleeping disorders and impairment of their concentration, nightmares, withdrawal, aggression, fear of unexpected sounds and movements, clinging behaviour, depression, inability to form close relationships, bed-wetting, and so on. These symptoms affect the way they relate to the world around them.

It is very difficult for Filipino children to understand the situation of armed conflict in their country. Often they try to find explanations for the killings, 'disappearances', or forced evacuations, by creating fantasies about them. Often, these imagined explanations are irrational, and even more frightening and confusing than what really happened. A child's explanation for the killing of her father, for example, may go like this: the day before the killing, the child was punished by the father for stealing a mango. She was very upset and wished she did not have a father. The next day the father is dead. The child concludes that he was killed because she wanted him dead; and feels very guilty because she thinks she *caused* the father's death.

As a general rule, a bereaved family does not want to expose the children to the pain of knowing what really occurred, especially where loved ones have died. For example, a mother may tell her children that their father is dead, but she still promises that they will see him again. She does not show her own pain about the loss of her husband in front of the children. The children are left confused. When they understand that death means that the dead person is not returning, they do not know what to think. Which is true: their own knowledge about death? or the assurance of their mother — the person they trust most in the world? Apart from the confusion, the children are not given the chance to grieve, nor are they provided with a model for how to express the feeling of loss.

Children of war face numerous emotional problems. One of the most difficult things for them is the question of trust. Some of them are even given 'cover names' and are totally confused about knowing to whom they can or cannot confide their real names. This is especially common when the parents are not around to tell them which name to use.

Another problem is that of parents' 'disappearance': the children are left with the fear that what happened to their parents will also happen to them some time in the future. Will their parents ever return? Are they still alive? Are they being hurt and tortured? Why did they leave the children behind, all alone?

Some children have witnessed massacres in which other children were killed. How can a child understand that? If other children can be killed, how can they themselves be safe? Others have been caught in cross-fire or bombardments, and sometimes been severely wounded. They are scared by every unexpected sound or movement. Many children see their parents being beaten up or even killed before their own eyes. If their parents are not able to protect and defend themselves, who is going to protect the child? Such children live in great fear and uncertainty.

And what about those children who have been forcibly evacuated from their homes? After being displaced from everything that is familiar to them, they are taken to an under-resourced evacuation centre where they may face hunger, as well as having to deal with many strange and unfamiliar people, also victims of forced evacuations. Lack of food and health care and hygienic conditions means that measles epidemics are common. What is the impact on a child of seeing other children dying all around them, sometimes in their hundreds?

The imprisonment of a parent also causes emotional problems. Some children refuse to go to school, because the gates and walls remind them of prison. How can a child make sense of the fact that his parents are in prison without committing any crime? Others have only known their parents separated — one in prison and the other at home — and do not understand the relationship between them after the incarcerated parent is released. When a father returns home from prison, a young child who has been used to sleeping with his mother finds himself sleeping alone – separated from his mother and replaced by an estranged father.

In addition to these psychological traumas — and it is very common for children to suffer a number of the problems described above — some children are also physically disabled for the rest of their lives.

The situation in which the children of war find themselves has been described as follows:

A healthy child, not only from a medical point of view, but also from a psychological and social perspective, is a child who is transparent. One can see what is going on inside the child, and the child does not have to hide his or her feelings and genuine thoughts. He or she knows that his or her family will protect him or her, and he or she has a network of relations and security systems which will protect him/her, in case his/her family fails to do so. The child of war is caught in a tangle of chaos.

The child without symptoms is probably worse off than the child with symptoms. At least the child with symptoms is trying to work his/her way out of the chaotic environment. Symptoms could take the form of an enhanced aggressiveness, regressive reactions and psychosomatic symptoms. Children with symptoms are able to allow others to see their fears, their protests and their sorrow. As long as there are symptoms, there is hope. What is far more serious is the child without symptoms. The shell is opaque, the child has lost his/her ability to communicate his/her emotions to the outside. Denial seems to be at the bottom of this reaction — denial of feelings of fear, anger or sorrow.[3]

These problems are very extensive in the Philippines. As of December 1988, there were 3,800,000 children who were victims of involuntary displacement; 144,000 children of political detainees; 4,681 children who had witnessed massacres; and 138,600 children orphaned by the 'disappearance' or killing of their parents.[4]

The government of the Philippines does almost nothing to help these children. Sometimes local government officials try to supply food and medicine for the evacuation centres — although they are never given enough resources to meet the needs, even when they sincerely try to carry out their jobs. However, psychological assistance is not available. The national government does not want to admit that children are victims of human-rights violations by its military — and often human-rights workers themselves are harassed or suffer similar violations.

Therapy at the Children's Rehabilitation Center

Much of the therapy work of the Children's Rehabilitation Center (CRC) in Davao City is done at home, with children and their parents (or with whoever takes responsibility for the children's welfare). The work is done at home, because that is where the children are, and where they have to function.[5] In addition, because the parents see the children so much and are so aware of their problems, they have to learn how to help the children deal with them.

Much of the therapy work is done through talking with the parents: one cannot help the children to change if the parents do not change too. The CRC staff member will question the parents or carers to get a sense of the child's problems and how the parents and child are dealing with them. Then the CRC staff member will make suggestions to encourage the parents to change any behaviour that is evidently working against the well-being of the children.

To return to our earlier example, where the mother told the children that the father was dead but they would see him again: the CRC staff member would explain to the mother that she can only help the children when she makes clear to them that the father is dead and so will never return. She also has to show her own grief about the loss of her husband in front of her children, to give them a model of grieving: children need that model in order to be able to give form to their own feelings. Only when the children's confusion is cleared up and they are given the space to grieve can the symptoms from the original trauma, as well as those caused by the confusion itself, disappear. As the mother does this, those behavioural problems in the children which are symptoms of psychological trauma have a chance to be resolved.

It is not enough to talk just with the parents: the CRC staff also work with the children to find out what is going on. To continue our example, the mother has told the CRC staff member that her oldest son has been stealing money from other people in the community and that this has given rise to anger against him. If the CRC staff member talked only with her, and not with the son, the suggested solution might revolve around getting the boy to stop stealing. However, working through painting, drama, and story telling, the CRC staff member finds out from the boy that he began stealing the money to give to his mother, so that she would not have to go out to work and leave him and his siblings alone, since he fears that she might not return either. Thus the stealing is a behavioural symptom of the psychological trauma that arose through his father's killing, and the child's confusion about his death.

It is only through working with all parties concerned — in this case the parents *and* the children — that solutions can be found. Clearing up the confusion and allowing the boy to grieve over the loss of his father, and supporting him in his grief, are essential if he is to work through his father's death in an effective way.

Creative Process Therapy

Creative Process Therapy (CPT) was developed in The Netherlands. It is a type of psycho-therapy using non-verbal media for individual expression. Five different media are used in CPT: visual arts, music, gardening, drama, and dance or movement.

CPT is built around how individuals relate to their immediate environment. For those working with visual arts, which is my area of training, the key factor is how a person relates in the therapy environment to handicraft material, to the tools available there, to the furniture in the room and how it is arranged, as well as to the therapist. The important thing in creative therapy is not the artistic quality of the product, but rather the manner in which it is made — in other words, the process.

There are several different ways in which people can feel themselves drawn to material. From the manner in which the patient is drawn to material and handles it, the therapist can make an 'appeal analysis'. Because the appeal of a medium has very much to do with the needs of the patient, the therapist can then draw up a 'needs hierarchy', derived from this analysis. If needs are seldom or never expressed, a defence mechanism is probably at work.

Before she can begin to experiment with those areas she considers 'dangerous', the patient needs to feel completely secure in the therapy situation. After the therapist has analysed the way in which the patient structures the environment, and how she creates unity in her relationship with it, it is possible to help to build up that sense of security. Play and 'pretend' situations often provide a feeling of security. Only when these conditions have been established can a creative process emerge, in which the patient can express existing needs and feelings, and gradually develop new understandings and possibilities for dealing with herself and the surrounding world.[6]

Planning to implement Creative Process Therapy at CRC

During the preparations for a residential workshop, the CRC staff suggested that I should attend it, and also conduct CPT sessions with the so-called 'live-in' children. These children were already at the centre, arriving a week before the workshop, to give them a chance to get used to the immediate environment of CRC. They had come from a centre in North Cotabato, a two-hour bus drive from Davao City, and were going to attend the whole six weeks of the workshop. The 'live-in children' would attend the CPT sessions in the morning, as well as the regular afternoon workshops.

My first reaction to this invitation was one of panic. How was I going to cope, without material, without knowing the language and without the same cultural background? Besides, the children in the group would have different cultures and languages among themselves, for they came from distinct ethnic groups and areas. What could the series of sessions achieve? How was I going to devise enough activities, given the limited resources? All I had was what I could find around the house. Furthermore, these children were also not at all used to expressing themselves through any form of visual arts. And all this, six mornings a week from 9 am to 12 noon — an extremely intensive schedule, requiring both the children and myself to be very concentrated for a relatively long period of time. (By contrast, in The Netherlands, group sessions last between only one and four hours a week!) In addition, I would not have time to make written reports, because in the afternoon I was to take part in the CRC sessions. This meant that I would be unable to plan the sessions very thoroughly, and would have to rely on my intuition and experience to ensure that they had some therapeutic value.

Despite all the questions and uncertainties, the fact that the children had managed to overcome linguistic and cultural barriers in order to establish contact with me, and that I really wanted to help them deal with their trauma, made me decide to face the challenge and give it a chance, to see it as an experiment, a learning experience. I decided that, rather than aiming for advanced therapeutic goals, the aim of the sessions would be to let the children have a pleasant time working together with visual arts. For children who had been through such traumatic experiences, I felt it important that they have a positive experience, doing something they might enjoy, in an environment that was caring and supportive. Positive experiences such as these can often help in building self-esteem — something these children were, understandably, seriously lacking.

The children

There were eight children in the group. The five 'live-in' children came from a house for child war victims in Kidapawan called 'Pagsagop Foundation'. The others spent the whole day at the centre because their mothers volunteered to do the cooking there. The children were between 7 and 17 years old and had all gone through some traumatic war experiences. Tata (10) and Gaga (7) had lost their parents and two sisters during a massacre in which the family members were hacked to death with bolo knives by fanatics from the Tad-Tad (which literally means 'chop-chop') vigilante group, and which the then 7-year old Tata witnessed. Their grandmother had tried to take care of them but, in view of her own poverty and the behavioural/emotional problems of the children, this was no longer possible. Royroy's (11) parents were arrested and 'disappeared'. Nonoy's (10) father was killed in front of their house, and his mother had left with Nonoy's older brother to restart her life on the northern island of Luzon; she had no intentions of letting Nonoy live with them after she remarried. Baby's (17) father was killed before her eyes. Weng (14) was gang-raped by a group of soldiers. Gigi (10) and Jun (12) were part of a group of internal refugees who had fled from their area because of years of massacres, hostage-taking, burning of houses, and bombardments by military and vigilante groups.

In addition, since human-rights lawyers use survivors to bring charges against the vigilante groups, military units, and individual soldiers, and because most of the children had witnessed such events — indeed, some were the sole witnesses of gross human rights violations by soldiers and vigilante groups — their own lives were in constant jeopardy.

The children came mostly from very poor families. After the parents were killed or 'disappeared', other family members tried to take care of them. But because none of the uncles, aunts, or grandparents had enough money to feed their own children, these already traumatised children were moved from one family to another. By the time the family caring for them actually asked for help, most of these children were seriously malnourished and felt totally abandoned. Indeed, the children all showed the symptoms of severe psychological trauma from the events mentioned above.

Results of the Creative Process Therapy

A CPT therapist working in a centre like CRC has to be far more creative than one working in a more economically developed country, such as The Netherlands. The therapist needs to be creative enough to find activities and materials appropriate to the stage in the patient's development at the particular moment of the session.

We had few resources for the children to use. I could only use areas in the house that the larger workshop was not using, and these changed from day to day. My entire range of materials and tools were scissors, glue, pencils, crayons, and paper. Once in a while, I had the money to buy coloured paper. So, I was obliged to find as many activities as possible that could be carried out with these materials, plus what I could find around the house, such as plants, seeds, cardboard boxes, and sea shells left from dinner.

Drawing was the children's only previous experience of working with visual arts, so it became central to our work. The children began with dozens of depictions of bombardments, killings, military encounters, and the like. They drew those things that had hurt them or that they feared most of all. They did this day by day, hour by hour, for around four and a half weeks. Only then, when this fear and aggression had been reduced sufficiently, did the children have room to express other feelings. They would then begin to see what other things were going on around them to be explored and perhaps even enjoyed; they started drawing children eating ice-cream, and houses, trees, fruits, kites, and lovely dresses.

The children's self-esteem improved greatly over this time, as I taught them techniques that were very simple but gave surprising and beautiful results. For example, I would have the children draw with glue on a piece of paper. After that they would cover their paper with fine sand, so that when they lifted it, they had a picture. For some of the children, it was a big surprise to find out they were actually good at something and genuinely appreciated by the people around them. This made it possible for some of them to start experimenting with the possibilities of a wider range of materials, including things that were to be found in the garden and house. Every time they succeeded in making something or finding something useful, they were proud and praised; this built up their self-esteem.

The CPT sessions were consolidated by the afternoon workshops, where the children would sing, play games and sports, and share in discussions about their experiences with the other children and staff members.

One example shows what this process meant for the children. One evening, Tata, for the first time in two months, was sitting in my lap. It was very cosy and we were not disturbed by other children. He told me he wanted to sing me a song, but that he was not a good singer. I replied that I would really like to hear the song anyway. He sang it while sitting in my lap and also held my arms around him and pinched me with his nails. It was very painful, but I didn't show it because I sensed that Tata was experimenting with being close to somebody again.

The case of Royroy

Royroy's parents had been community organisers. One night, they were arrested by men in military uniforms. Royroy was the only child present in the house when this happened. He claims that he recognised the armed men and can identify them. His parents were found dead the next morning.

Like all the other children in the group, Royroy started with drawing. He produced drawing after drawing full of little human figures carrying guns, shooting at each other and at helicopters. Royroy was usually present in his own drawings, fighting with the good guys against the bad guys. The bad guys were from the military unit that took away Royroy's parents. It seemed as if Royroy wanted to take revenge. His depictions were very detailed and it was clear that he had a talent for drawing and composition. He worked quietly and had little conversation with the other children in the group. I was ignored by him most of the time and Royroy pulled away if he was touched. He seemed to have little self-esteem and to be shy.

I let Royroy work in peace. I didn't express any expectations, just provided him with enough paper for all his drawings. I also told him that I thought he had a talent for art-work. That comment made him look me straight in the eyes with delight, but he withdrew again almost immediately.

Slowly I introduced other techniques which the children could use in their drawings, such as the use of glue and sand described above. Royroy turned out to be very creative. He also seemed to enjoy the sessions more and more. He was the first one who had the idea of using other materials that he found in the garden, such as grass and leaves. From there, he made the step to three-dimensional art work, like folding paper in the form of a boat. His work continued to be detailed — his paper boat had a sail, a net, and fishermen — and beautiful. The other children and I all showed our appreciation of Royroy's work. He gradually become less shy and started to show me things of which he was particularly proud.

One day in the fourth week, Royroy showed me a picture of two armies fighting each other. He pointed out where he was in the drawing and than he pointed at another figure fighting at his side and said that it was me. He had accepted me and even felt that I was on his side.

After that, Royroy started drawing other things like houses, trees, and children with ice-creams. His pictures about war retreated into the background. He smiled more, talked with the other children, was obviously proud of his art-work and stopped ignoring me. Even so, he was more shy than the other children.

In the meantime, Royroy had saved all his pocket money and, on the last day of the programme, he bought a toy gun and a toy knife. These must have given him a feeling of security and possibly power, as he walked around sure of himself, looking people straight in the face, and talking to others. Indeed, these toy items seemed to give him his self-esteem.

Of course, Royroy still has a long way to go, but he has gained some things from the CPT sessions: he has started to connect with others, feeling again that there are people who support him and who are on his side. He has had the experience of being good at something, realising that he is creative and that he is appreciated by other people. He has regained some self-esteem and was able to express some of his vengeful feelings. In the future, he may be able to use his obvious creative talents, in dealing with other events in his life.

Conclusion

Armed conflict has a disproportionate impact on the children in the areas affected by it. While traumatised children are initially a by-product of violence, eventually they threaten the future stability of any community, since they have no way to deal with feelings triggered by the war, except through disturbed behaviour. This itself reduces social stability, making the entire community more vulnerable to outside pressures. It is crucial to any development process to help children to overcome the traumatic experiences they may have suffered, in a way that supports and validates them.

While the experiment in Davao City was not formally designed, nor were daily accounts kept, empirical evidence suggests that CPT is a tool that might be of very great use in rehabilitation and development. It may be worth designing a more formal experimental process for comparable situations, so that the potential application of this therapeutic approach may be more fully evaluated. Similarly, although this article points to the cross-cultural and cross-lingual capabilities of the approach, further studies are required.

While it will not be possible universally to apply CPT in precisely the same form as it is implemented in The Netherlands, I am convinced that the basic principles and ideas behind it will fit any child in any setting — as long as the indigenous culture and situation are specifically taken into account and incorporated into the therapy process. Furthermore, it is essential to have local staff with previous experience in the use of creative activities for therapy purposes, who can be trained in the use of CPT; this will help to ensure that it enriches any existing indigenous therapeutic models. For example, the CRC staff members knew what they wanted to learn; they were keen to understand why certain activities had the impact they did on particular children. If there is no such experience among the local staff, the danger is that this Western therapeutic approach will predominate over indigenous initiatives, and so fail to meet the needs of the patients themselves. For this reason too, it is essential that the trainee participants and the trainer share a language that they all understand and speak fluently.[7]

In terms of development policy, the funding and training of local people in CPT could offer beneficial long-term results. Working for the mental health of the children of today should contribute to building a mentally healthier generation of adults in the future.

Notes

1 Thanks to Kim Scipes for his assistance in preparing this article.

2 For a detailed interview with Beth Marcelino, co-founder of the CRC, see Joseph Collins: 'Interview with Dr Elizabeth Marcelino, Director, Children's Rehabilitation Center, Manila', in *The Philippines: Fire on the*

Rim, San Francisco: Institute for Food and Development Policy: 291, 292 (1989). Although CRC was first established in Manila, it has expanded to include regional offices in Davao City on Mindanao, the Bicol region in the far southern tip of Luzon, and in Bacolod and Iloilo in the Western Visayas region. This account is based on my experiences in CRC-Davao City.

3 Jasmin E. Acuna: 'Children of war: state of the art' in Elizabeth Protacio-Marcelino (ed.): *First International Seminar-Workshop on Children in Crisis: Working Paper*, Quezon City, Philippines: Children's Rehabilitation Center: 175, 183-184 (1989).

4 These data were cited from an article by Rolando Rodriguez in *Kalingangan*, a magazine of the Institute for Religion and Culture, in Sylvia Estrada-Claudio, José F Bartolomé and Grace Aguiling-Dalisay: 'Pilot study on children in crisis' in Protacio-Marcelino (op. cit.): 71, 73.

5 While most of the work done in Western Europe and the United States with torture victims and refugees has been valuable, it differs from work in a war-ravaged area: in war zones, children remain subject to future violence, and so much of our work, by necessity, focuses on enabling past victims to deal successfully with their still-violent environment.

6 J. Houben, H. Smitskamp and J. te Velde (eds.): *The Creative Process*, part I, 'Applications in Therapy and Education', Culemborg, Netherlands: Phaedon (1989).

7 Assuming that CPT trainees have some background in rehabilitation work and are familiar with non-verbal forms of therapy, my experience suggests that a two-week formal training programme (based on a six-hour working day) should be followed with between 15 and 30 therapy sessions under supervision: at the end of this, trainees should be able to transfer their skills to other colleagues, though they may need further back-up in teaching and instruction methods. It is also important that trainees are monitored regularly, throughout the process. The trainer will also need time to get a feel for the culture and for indigenous art forms in preparation for the training; and adequate time needs to be built into the process for assessment sessions and final evaluation. In all, a complete CPT training would require between 28 and 43 weeks, exclusive of all the written and other documentary work entailed.

The author

Hàns Buwalda is a Creative Process Therapist. When she wrote this article, she was a volunteer, working with the Children's Rehabilitation Center in the Philippines, an organisation that is developing a treatment and rehabilitation programme for children psychologically traumatised by war experiences.

This article was first published in *Development in Practice*, Volume 4, Number 1, in 1994.

Training indigenous workers in mental-health care

Jane Shackman and Jill Reynolds

Introduction

Hàns Buwalda's article, 'Children of war in the Philippines' [reprinted in this volume], describes some of the emotional problems of children in the Philippines, traumatised by political violence, and relates her introduction of Creative Process Therapy at the Children's Rehabilitation Center in Davao City. It raises interesting issues concerning the modification and application of a Western therapeutic model to a South-East Asian country experiencing long-term conflict.

We would like to explore this further in relation to the kinds of training programme that are currently being developed in former Yugoslavia and other areas of war or civil war. The aim is to train workers from ethnic minorities in mental-health care and counselling skills, to enable them to work with refugees and displaced people who have been subjected to war and extreme brutality, including detention, rape, and torture. All will have been affected by these experiences, and some may have been seriously traumatised. The training programmes and subsequent mental-health work often take place in over-crowded and under-resourced refugee camps, or in situations where fighting still rages, and basic needs for safety, food, and shelter can barely be met, let alone social, emotional and mental-health needs.

As trainers with experience in the field of refugee rehabilitation, we were approached by a British worker who had just been appointed as a Training Officer for a non-governmental organisation (NGO) in Croatia. Her main role would be to train Serbo-Croatian speaking workers in counselling skills and mental-health care for their work with displaced people from Bosnia. A psychiatric social worker herself, she had years of experience in the mental-health field, in various different settings — but she had no experience as a trainer, nor in work with refugees. She was clearly anxious about her role, and phoned us for advice two weeks before going to Croatia.

Her questions to us included the following: How do I plan and run appropriate training courses? What are the participants going to want to know? How do I find an effective way to share my own skills? In an attempt to address some of these issues, we offer this article to everyone working in similar areas of conflict.

First thoughts

If you are feeling anxious about the limitations of your own skills and experiences in an unfamiliar context, remember that this may be how the participants on your training courses will be feeling. If you feel daunted by the task ahead, this may well reflect some of the fears of those whom you are setting out to train in mental-health work.

We suggest that addressing participants' own concerns and anxieties is a good way to start such a training course. It will enable you to identify more clearly their training requirements, and increase their confidence in expressing and asserting their needs.

It will be important to combine your own therapeutic approaches with the cultural frameworks and ways of working familiar to participants, so you need to become as familiar as possible (as quickly as possible!) with the local cultures, values, and situation, and take account of these in your training programmes and models of work. The participants on your training courses will be a rich source of information and knowledge, and they should be able to work with you to adapt ideas into culturally appropriate ways of working.

The selection of trainees

The trainees' own experiences, knowledge, and status within their communities will affect how they are seen and are able to function. Selection needs to take account of their standing and status within their communities, if they are to be trusted and well received. Primary heath-care workers or community health promoters, for example, will usually be known and trusted, and may be possible candidates for training courses. You may have little control over selection of trainees when you first arrive, but ideally you should introduce a sensitive selection procedure. Clearly the existing knowledge and skill-level of trainees will guide the design and process of your course.

Emotional impact of the work

In training people to work with refugees and displaced people, you need to address the emotional impact of the work on the trainees. No matter what ideas, training modules, exercises, and frameworks you bring, it is important to help participants understand and come to terms with their own mixed feelings about the work they are going to undertake. They are likely to have feelings of impotence and inadequacy, even sometimes of despair, as well as hopes, commitment, energy, and creative ideas. Acknowledging such emotions

does not form a separate 'topic' in training, but runs throughout the entire course. You need to build in opportunities for participants to reflect on and talk about their own feelings about the work, and indeed about the training exercises you have asked them to do, and the feelings these may stir up.

The aim is to help workers to deal with their feelings of being overwhelmed or distressed. Remember that they are intimately involved with the conflict in ways that you are not. They are likely to share many of the losses and traumas of those they will be working with. That gives them both a unique strength, in understanding and empathising, and a vulnerability, in that the work may leave their own sorrows exposed.

In addition, clients can be very demanding, angry with workers who are unable to provide what they want, and jealous of workers' paid employment. The workers will have responsibilities that are new to them, such as assessing clients for propensity to suicide — and this can be a heavy burden.

Mental-health work is often painful and draining. The training should help workers to recognise their own emotional needs, and support them in their right to ask for help themselves. One Bosnian worker in the UK works all hours of the day and night, so that (she says) she can keep her feelings of distress at bay. She receives no continuous support or supervision. This is one way of dealing with painful feelings that threaten to overwhelm us, but workers should be given opportunities to seek and receive support from others.

There are many ways in which you can pay attention to the trainees' emotional responses, and you will have to make judgements about how far deliberately to encourage self-disclosure in the groups with whom you work. If people have been working hard to keep their feelings of distress at bay, they will not welcome being stripped of their defences. Exercises and discussions which give participants the opportunity to 'put themselves in the position of the client' can be a gentle way to give recognition to participants' own needs for support.

An exercise on 'Asking for help' (Open University 1993) draws attention to the anxieties and loss of control that people often feel in seeking help.

Participants work in threes and each person is asked to think of a relationship with which there were difficulties. Whether or not they sought help in improving the relationship at the time, what difficulties could there have been for them in asking someone outside the relationship for help? When all three have discussed what might have made it hard to ask for help, they are then asked to consider what additional factors might make it difficult for refugees, or those who have been traumatised, to ask for help.

You can vary this exercise by making 'difficulties in working relationships' into the focus. It is in either case likely to give rise to some acknowledgement of trainees' own needs, and their feelings of ambivalence in seeking help.

Often clients will not talk immediately about emotional problems, but may discuss more practical concerns. Trainees can be helped to attend sensitively to these demands, to build up trust first, before trying to open up more emotional topics for discussion.

On-going support for workers

In times of conflict, normal support networks are disrupted or broken completely, and new ones may need to be built. Training courses give an opportunity to start this process. Allow time for trainees to discuss what kind of support they need, and how it could be provided. They may be able to meet together in smaller groups on a regular basis, if they work in nearby geographical areas; or they may ask the organisations employing them to establish a support or supervision structure. You will probably need to back up such requests by holding your own discussions with employing organisations. Burn-out is a real factor in this type of work: after a while workers themselves can become depressed, bored, or discouraged (van der Veer 1992), and support networks for them need to be established early on.

Create a safe atmosphere

If you can create an atmosphere of trust and openness, where trainees feel comfortable enough to share their anxieties, fears, vulnerabilities, hopes, and ideas, and to acknowledge the emotional impact of the work on themselves, they will be prepared to take risks in learning and trying out new techniques in working with clients. If you create a safe atmosphere, trainees will be able to make better use of any structured activities and exercises which you introduce, and to practise, challenge, and adapt new skills.

How can such an atmosphere be created? Think about how you will introduce the training course, and the way in which you intend to work. Proper introductions are important, and the chance to 'warm up' through non-threatening activities. We often use an exercise which combines elements of introductions and warm up.

Ask each participant to tell the group about his or her name, and what it means. Each person speaks in turn for a few minutes only. Participants will decide for themselves how much they want to share at this stage. If you start, you can set the tone for others. The exercise gives opportunities for people to talk about their ethnicity, family history, religion. It is surprising how much a name can mean to its owner and how quickly a few words on this can give others in the group a glimpse, revealing more of the whole person.

You can use warming-up exercises for a few minutes at the beginning of each new session: something light-hearted before serious business begins, and a chance for individuals to feel connected again with the group. Talking about something which they have enjoyed recently, or a memory of the last session, are other ways of giving each person a moment to say something at the start of a new session. Giving each person a turn is less embarrassing for them than if you put pressure on an individual to speak in general discussion.

Exercises can help people to think about issues from a different angle, and should promote discussion. A good approach is to move from individual work, to paired conversation, to small-group discussion. If people have had a chance to note down their own thoughts first, they are more likely to feel confident enough to talk to one another, and then to enter into group discussion. Encourage everyone to participate, using their own experiences and ideas, and value all their contributions. Acknowledge and deal with the emotions that are evoked. Give plenty of opportunity for participants to use their own case-studies and examples in their paired and group discussions.

Training methods

You may find that the way of training which we are advocating is very different from what trainees expect. Perhaps they hope you will present lectures, or teach more formally; whereas we are suggesting training that is experiential and participatory, with you in the role of facilitator rather than teacher. We believe this can be negotiated with the group, by explaining your training methods and the reasons why you use them. But you may need to make some concession to your trainees' preferences. This could be by giving some short prepared inputs, perhaps summarising learning and discussion from earlier sessions. It is hard for people to adapt to unfamiliar learning styles, and you will need to take this into account.

Participation is one of the keys to a successful training course. We believe that people 'learn by doing', and by reflecting on their own work. You can achieve a high level of participation by starting where they and their communities are. The theoretical underpinning for this approach comes from the ideas of Paulo Freire on popular education. Freire's literacy

programmes for slum dwellers in Brazil involved people in group efforts to identify their own problems, to analyse critically the cultural and socio-economic roots of the problems, and to develop strategies to effect positive changes in their lives and in their communities. In effect, people teach themselves in dialogue with each other. Paulo Freire's advice on this process is relevant:

Every human being is capable of looking critically at his world in a dialogic encounter with others ... In this process, the old paternalistic teacher/student relationship is overcome. A peasant can facilitate this process for his neighbour more effectively than a 'teacher' brought in from the outside. Each man wins back his own right to say his own word, to name the world. (Freire 1972)

While trainees on your courses may hope that you are coming as an 'expert', to impart solutions to the problems with which they are grappling, you are more likely to be struck by the fact that you are working in a country, culture, and situation where your knowledge is limited. You may wonder whether your experience and skills have relevance. It is important to clarify your role early on: you do have expertise and techniques to share, but as a trainer you are there to help trainees to recognise and draw on their own resources and skills. You are there to help the group to tap their own wealth of experiences and creative ideas. We find that case-studies and role-play help this process.

In small groups of four or five, trainees can think of a real or hypothetical client they are worried about, or you can present a prepared case-study. After reading the outline of the case, and particularly the presenting problem, ask trainees to discuss in their groups (1) what do you feel?, (2) what do you think?, (3) what are your first steps going to be?, (4) how are you going to approach the client, what are you going to say? After discussion, trainees can role-play the start of the interview with the client.

Role-play should be seen not as a test, but as an opportunity for trainees to practise different ways of intervening, and to receive feedback about their impact and ideas about other approaches. Those in the role-play and the observers can swap places to try out different strategies. Linked with discussion, planning, and review, and done in a supportive environment, role-play can be one of the most effective ways of learning.

Cultural considerations

There are likely to be considerable cultural differences between yourself as trainer, and your trainees, just as there may well be differences within your group of trainees, and between the trainees and the clients with whom they will be working. You cannot assume that trainees understand everything of their clients' backgrounds and values, just because they are members of the same wider community. An examination of cultural expectations, values, strengths, and differences on training courses is important, in order to sensitise participants to their own cultural norms and biases in relation to their clients, and to encourage them to build on the inherent cultural and community strengths in coping with losses, crises, and traumas.

Here is an exercise which can open up some discussion on different cultural values.

Participants first note their individual responses to the following instructions:

• *List six values passed on to you by parents or care-givers.*
• *How did your parents or care-givers make you aware of important values?*
• *Circle the values that you consider to be peculiar to your cultural, ethnic, or racial group.*
• *Place a tick next to the values that you still adhere to and a cross next to those that you no longer adhere to.*

Participants then work in groups of three to discuss their responses (Christensen 1992).

Participants may be surprised at values which are held in common, despite cultural differences, or at different interpretations of what values mean in terms of behaviour. They can recognise that most values are passed on by example and non-verbal means. Participants will usually identify the dangers of imposing their own value system. If the group you are working with share a common cultural background, this exercise brings out differences in emphasis, interpretation, and upbringing. This is helpful in cautioning trainees against assuming that they and their clients share common values and aspirations.

Again, opportunities for participants to think about their individual responses and to work first in small groups are important in giving everyone a chance to be heard, and allowing differences to emerge.

There is still a risk of inadvertently imposing your own cultural bias and value system in your powerful position as a trainer. It is not always easy to recognise your own cultural 'spectacles' (Finlay and Reynolds 1987). For example, your own professional social work training, if rooted in Western, Anglo-Saxon, and Christian values, has probably tended to focus on personal, rather than collective, achievement, fulfilment and satisfaction, and to have valued independent thought and action. But the individual perspective is not always central. Be prepared to have your own assumptions challenged.

An awareness of gender-linked differences is vital. How men and women are seen in their culture, and their investments in it, are not necessarily the same. Their responses to pain and losses, how they process these, and their willingness to express emotions may differ. Therefore you should think about how you might handle mixed training groups of men and women, and how you will deal with issues that may generate different reactions and responses according to gender. Sexual crimes, such as rape during civil conflict, would be a case in point. It may be helpful for participants to work in same-sex groups on some topics, so that people have the chance to work out their ideas before sharing them with the mixed group.

Course content

So far we have mainly discussed the process of the group, and methods of training. We now consider some of the topics which we think you could usefully include (Reynolds and Shackman 1993).

Theories of loss and bereavement are central to work with refugees and displaced people. They will have suffered personal losses: the deaths of family and friends, the destruction of their homes, the loss of belongings; and abstract losses: certainly the loss of their familiar life-style, and maybe the loss of beliefs, ideologies, and hopes for the future. They will be uncertain whether some of these losses are permanent or temporary. They will be struggling to make sense of what has happened, to give meaning to the appalling events. An understanding of loss and bereavement can help trainees in their assessments. But you need to take into account that different societies have different ways of dealing with massive losses and grief, and have their own mourning rituals and rites of passage. These are often more collective and community-based than in Western society. Training should help trainees to recognise community responses and strengths, so they can build on these in their work. Many refugees and displaced people feel guilty about the deaths of loved ones, and have been unable to grieve for them.

Crisis intervention is another theoretical framework which can be useful, so trainees can look at the more normal stages of transition in a person's life (such as adolescence, marriage, unemployment, old age), and how they are differently affected by unexpected crises or changes. Times of crisis are difficult and painful, but sometimes can present opportunities for positive, as well as negative, changes.

Training in *assessment skills* is a useful tool, in helping to identify what a client may need, and who needs additional help. Trainees can be helped to distinguish between 'normal' distress and more serious mental-health problems, so they can decide when to refer on for psychiatric help (a tricky decision, when specialist services are likely to be scarce). Trainees will be in a better position than you to know what is regarded as 'normal' and 'abnormal' in their own culture, and this should be openly discussed. The stigma of mental illness may prevent many people from coming for help. Workers can find ways to encourage people to ask for help after extreme suffering, without its being seen as illness, or weakness. A checklist for assessing suicide risk in clients can be useful, as can an analysis of the uses (and sometimes abuses) of psychotropic medication. You will want to raise trainees' awareness of the more vulnerable members of the community: for example, children, particularly those who are unaccompanied; women on their own; the elderly; and those with a previous history of mental illness.

An understanding of some of the possible effects of torture and trauma will help trainees to make accurate assessments: nightmares, lack of concentration, and flashbacks of traumatic events are often experienced by survivors of torture and trauma, but are not an indication of mental ill-health unless they are seriously affecting the person's ability to cope.

Workers can reassure clients that these kinds of symptom are to be expected after a traumatic experience. If the person is unable to manage daily living tasks and interactions, this is a better indication than symptoms alone that a person is at risk and that extra help is needed (Summerfield 1992). Often members of the surrounding community will be able to identify those whom they see as 'not managing'.

Counselling skills and supportive, attentive, and non-judgemental listening can be developed by practice and role-plays. Trainees can choose or be given case-studies and can practise, for example, how to approach and talk to a person who is withdrawn and very depressed; how to listen and respond to someone who is extremely distressed and agitated; how to work with a client's anger and bitter hopelessness about the future.

Exercises and discussions that enable trainees to clarify their role and limitations are helpful. This was a topic that took up considerable time on a recent training course which one of us helped to run for Serbo-Croatian speaking workers in the UK, who worked with Bosnian refugees in exile. They were beset by demands from clients, colleagues, and their employing agencies. Becoming clear about their role and asserting what expectations they could, or could not, meet gave them confidence to say 'No' when necessary.

Other useful topics could include *problem-solving techniques, interpreting skills, community development*, and *working with women who have been raped*. (Such women are unlikely to come forward for 'rape counselling', but might welcome the chance to be medically examined, and later may want to talk about their experiences or meet with other women who have suffered in similar ways.) Developing *group-work skills* is extremely useful, where numbers affected by violence and trauma are large, and where there is a more collective approach to dealing with grief and loss. People can gain confidence and strength from sharing experiences and supporting each other (Blackwell 1989; Shackman and Tribe 1989). Guatemalan women in Mexico City who met as a self-help group realised that they had all been going around thinking 'I'm crazy', when really they were suffering the effects of severe political repression and isolation (Finlay and Reynolds 1987).

You will probably think of many other topics: in developing the contents of training courses, you can make full use of your own professional training and skills. We suggest that you list all the topics you could cover, and what you think trainees may want to learn. Make up or adapt exercises to allow participants to try out new skills and techniques, and be clear about the teaching points you want to make. You probably won't use all of them and, once you find out the needs of your trainees, you will have to adapt your plans accordingly. You will feel more confident if you know you have some ideas prepared: a selection you can dip into, a varied and filling menu from which you and the participants can taste samples. You will learn about new approaches and ways of working from the trainees themselves.

Constructing an interesting programme

Working with clients who may be traumatised and experiencing mental-health problems can be draining, and so can training courses dealing with these issues. Having a variety of topics and exercises will enable you to vary the pace and the atmosphere. Sometimes you might want to lighten the tone. Warm-up exercises can be fun, and can have useful teaching points. If you have access to video and/or slides, they too are useful teaching tools, which give participants a break from concentrating on themselves. Prepared hand-outs provide reminders of key points covered. Summaries, feedback, and evaluation sessions at the end of each day will reinforce what has been done, highlight what participants have found useful, and disclose what the gaps are.

During the training course for Serbo-Croatian speaking workers we spent time reading poems, singing folk and popular songs from Bosnia, telling jokes, and drawing (they produced some vivid group pictures representing 'Being a Good Listener'). All these activities helped to build a strong group identity, and created a good atmosphere of trust and openness, in which many difficult issues were discussed and tackled.

We recommend that participants evaluate each training course at the end, to help you to develop other courses. Ask for comments on various aspects, including your own style: if you can get people to write down responses before you all disperse, you should get some honest feedback.

Be prepared for the unexpected

Quite often trainers face the uncertainty of being unsure how long the training courses will be, or who will attend them. It is likely that you will be required to run a variety of different courses for both inexperienced and more experienced workers. In addition, you may perhaps be asked to act as a consultant to groups or teams of workers. This is a different role, and you need to clarify what you are being asked to do. Every training course is different, but we hope we have given you some useful general guidelines.

If it is possible to work alongside another trainer, do so, preferably someone who shares language and culture with the participants. It is always more productive and creative to work with a co-trainer, to plan courses together, to deal with difficult situations, to support each other. You will need to spend time developing a working relationship with a co-trainer, and even then things will not always go smoothly, but it is time well spent (Reynolds and Shackman, forthcoming).

Developing a model of training for the future

We hope we have given you some ideas and confidence to get started. As you continue your preparation, it is worth reading accounts of training programmes developed in Latin America which provide models of how work can continue to have effects long after your own relatively brief appointment is over. The self-help group we have already mentioned with Guatemalans in Mexico City developed a core group of female mental-health promoters who continued to work with refugee women and children, and to run workshops for others for some years after the initial project (Ball 1991). A training model that reaches respected members of a community can have a 'multiplier' effect in ensuring that skills and appropriate methodologies are passed on to others.

It is important for the NGOs implementing training programmes in mental health to integrate this work into longer-term development projects. All too often, such work is part of a crisis response, when what is needed is commitment to supporting psycho-social programmes over a period, to give continuity with wider-ranging health and community-development plans. If you can raise these issues with your NGO at an early stage, you may be able to ensure that your work has far-reaching effects on the life of the community.

References

Ball, C., 1991, 'When broken-heartedness becomes a political issue', in T. Wallace and C. March (eds.): *Changing Perceptions: Writings on Gender and Development*, Oxford: Oxfam Publications.

Blackwell, R.D., 1989, *The Disruption and Reconstruction of Family, Network and Community Systems Following Torture, Organised Violence and Exile*, London: The Medical Foundation for the Care of Victims of Torture.

Buwalda, H., 1994, 'Children of war in the Philippines', *Development in Practice*, 4 (1): 3-12.

Christensen, C.P., 1992, 'Training for cross-cultural social work with immigrants, refugees and minorities, a course model', in Ryan (ed.): *Social Work with Immigrants and Refugees*, New York: Haworth.

Finlay, R. and J. Reynolds, 1987, *Social Work and Refugees: A Handbook on Working with People in Exile in the UK*, Cambridge: National Extension College/Refugee Action.

Freire, P., 1972, *Pedagogy of the Oppressed*, Harmondsworth: Penguin.

Open University, 1993, *Roles and Relationships: Perspectives on Practice in Health and Welfare*, (K663), Workbook 2, 'Focusing on Roles and Relationships', Milton Keynes: Open University.

Reynolds, J. and J. Shackman, 1993, 'Refugees and Mental Health: Issues for Training', *Mental Health News*.

Reynolds, J. and J. Shackman (forthcoming), *Partnership in Training and Practice with Refugees*.

Shackman, J. and R. Tribe, 1989, *A Way Forward: A Group for Refugee Women*, London: Medical Foundation for the Care of Victims of Torture.

Summerfield, D., 1992, *Addressing Human Response to War and Atrocity: An Overview of Major Themes*, London: Medical Foundation for the Care of Victims of Torture.

van der Veer, G., 1992, *Counselling and Therapy with Refugees: Psychological Problems of Victims of War, Torture and Repression*, Chichester: Wiley.

The authors

Jill Reynolds is a lecturer at the Open University (UK) in the School of Health, Welfare and Community Education. Her previous experience includes providing training for para-social workers and community workers from Vietnam and other refugee groups. She has developed teaching programmes on refugees for social work professional training.

Jane Shackman is a training coordinator at the Medical Foundation for the Care of Victims of Torture, specialising in the needs of refugees. She has developed training on the problems of refugees for various local authorities, aimed at social-work staff and teachers.

This article was first published in *Development in Practice*, Volume 4, Number 2, in 1994.

The United Nations speaks out on forced evictions

Miloon Kothari

Introduction

Perhaps the most crucial yet widely misunderstood aspect of human rights concerns international action pertaining to these rights. On the one hand, it is seen as an instrument with which the United States and other Western countries are seeking to browbeat the nations of the Third World. On the other, the more realistic course of enforcing human rights through the United Nations system is overworked or deliberately ignored.

This is noticeable when poor and vulnerable sections of society face crises of sustenance and survival. The widest-known instance concerns large-scale displacement, eviction, dispossession, and forced migration of literally millions of people around the world – usually in the developing world, though often perpetrated and initiated at the instances of global institutions like the World Bank, and the donor agencies of industrialised nations.

Forced evictions, the uprooting of people and communities from their homes against their will, have become a recurring phenomenon in all regions of the world. In many countries, forced evictions are a routine event; but their impact of dislocation and devastation is hard to imagine, let alone assess.

However, spurred on by spirited NGO involvement, and influenced by ground-breaking work of the UN human rights bodies, the concerns, studies, and resolutions now emanating from the UN human rights programme are markedly different in tone and content from those that characterised the 1970s and 1980s.[1] There is now a critical and timely understanding of the structural inequities that contribute to the prevalence of phenomena such as forced evictions. Critical for all those struggling with daily survival issues is the attempt to 'blur' the distinction between economic, social, and cultural rights on the one hand, and civil and political rights on the other. Such an artificial distinction has overshadowed and often undermined any meaningful work in the field of international human rights. The recent holistic approach is particularly timely, given that the USA, even under the Clinton Administration, continues to play down the importance, recognition, and ratification of international instruments that confer economic, social, and cultural rights.

The last few years have witnessed rapid developments. The work of the UN Sub-Commission on Prevention of Discrimination and the Protection of Minorities (henceforth the Sub-Commission), a sister body of the UN Commission on Human Rights charged with carrying out studies and making recommendations to the Commission for further action, is noteworthy. The pioneering work of its member, Danilo Turk, UN Special Rapporteur on the Realisation of Economic, Social and Cultural rights, has brought these rights into clear focus. His second progress report was devoted entirely to documenting the adverse impact of economic adjustment policies, particularly those fashioned by the IMF and the World Bank, on the realisation of economic, social, and cultural rights.[2] One of the recommend-ations – for the need to draft guidelines on economic adjustment policies set within the human rights framework – is currently under consideration at the UN Centre for Human Rights.

The right to adequate housing

In August 1992 the Sub-Commission on Human Rights appointed Justice Rajindar Sachar as the UN Special Rapporteur on the realisation of the right to adequate housing. In his Working Paper, Justice Sachar tried to identify the root causes for the prevalence of housing crises, including the failure of government policies; discrimination in the housing sphere; structural adjustment pro-grammes and debt, poverty, and the depriva-tion of means; and forced evictions.[3]

The working paper was acclaimed both by members of the Sub-Commission and by a range of NGOs active at the Sub-Commission on issues as diverse as health, environment, poverty, and torture. What was particularly appreciated was the attempt to identify a series of violations to which the right to housing is routinely subject, and to project the need for sustained work on such 'preventative' rights, so as to gain a grasp on the structural causes for the decline of housing and living conditions worldwide. In 1993 Justice Sachar presented his first Progress Report, in which he focused on the nature of government obligations regarding the right to housing. This has contributed to furthering the understanding of how economic, social, and cultural rights can be realised, and what actions governments are expected to undertake and what processes they are supposed to halt, so that these rights can be gained and retained.[4]

The Committee on Economic, Social, and Cultural Rights, the UN treaty body which is charged with monitoring compliance with the International Covenant of Economic, Social and Cultural Rights (ICESCR),[5] has since 1991 been giving legal interpretation, in the form of General Comments, to the various articles in the ICESCR that contain the principal rights on which the covenant is based: Health, Education, Food, Housing and so on. The first General Comment on a specific right, the right to adequate housing, was adopted in December 1991.[6]

The foundation of this document is the understanding that all human rights are integrally linked, and that the right to housing *'should not be interpreted in a narrow or restrictive sense which equates it with, for example, the shelter provided by merely having a roof over one's head, or views shelter exclusively as a commodity. Rather it should be seen as the right to live somewhere in security and dignity.'* In addition, the Committee has begun to argue for new instruments, such as an Optional Protocol to the ICESCR.[7] Such a mechanism would finally allow individuals and groups whose rights under the Covenant have been violated to submit formal complaints to the Committee, seeking redress and compens-ation for such infringements.[8]

These recent developments in the UN are in large part a result of the insight and inform-ation that has been generated by NGOs, many from the Third World. On the issue of forced evictions, for example, information from a range of NGOs from across the world helped to convince the UN to adopt resolutions on the subject.

The Forced Evictions Resolution

One reflection of the trend within the UN towards a more holistic view of human rights is the ground-breaking resolutions and pronouncements addressing the phenom-enon of forced evictions.

Recognising that forced evictions are not limited to large-scale development projects and so-called 'urban redevelopment' and 'urban beautification' plans, the UN now admits that 'forced evictions' encompass a range of more insidious phenomena that result from the ravages of insensitive and misguided development policies, and have a deleterious effect on the skills, identity, and sheer survival of people and communities.

The Commission on Human Rights

In March 1993 the UN Commission on Human Rights adopted a resolution entitled 'Forced Evictions', urging governments immediately to desist from all processes that lead to the large-scale displacements of people and communities from their homes, a practice which it terms as a 'gross violation of human rights, in particular the right to adequate housing'.[9] The Commission defined the phenomenon of forced evictions as *'the involuntary removal of persons, families and groups from their homes and communities, resulting in increased levels of homelessness and in inadequate living conditions'*.

This historic resolution, from the UN's leading human rights policy-making body, consisting of 53 governments, provides a major instrument for all groups struggling against the widespread and growing phenomenon of forced evictions. The adoption of the resolution comes after a three-year effort at the UN in Geneva by a Mexico-based NGO, Habitat International Coalition (HIC), which has been leading the NGO initiative within the UN on the issues of housing rights and evictions. HIC has been backed by a growing network of NGOs and CBOs across the world that have provided information to HIC and have been sending activists to testify to the various UN Human Rights Bodies.

In the various submissions to the UN and the various global surveys of past and pending forced evictions prepared by HIC, examples such as the Sardar Sarovar project on the Narmada river in India have been used to illustrate the folly of indulging in projects involving large-scale evictions.[10] In addition to the evictions resulting from mega-projects, many more insidious processes have prevailed across the world, ranging from lack of livelihood opportunities, increased insecurity from communal strife, the changes in modes of agricultural production partly affecting small farmers, and extraction of natural resources to meet growing markets in urban areas for the consumer needs of elite classes. In India alone, some analysts put the figure, just for the large dam projects, at an astounding 20 to 30 million people displaced since the country gained independence in 1947.[11]

For countries going through stages of 'structural adjustment', such processes are bound to accelerate. This is partly a result of the severe erosion of the rights of access to basic social resources, caused by reductions in government spending. When one adds the impact of rising land prices in an unbridled speculative market and the additional burden of paying for civic services (electricity, water, sanitation) on the already limited purchasing power of the majority, the prospects are ominous indeed.[12]

The resolution urges governments to *'confer legal security of tenure to all persons currently threatened with eviction and to adopt all necessary measures giving full protection against forced evictions, based upon effective participation, consultation and negotiation with affected persons or groups'*. It admits that *'forced evictions and homelessness intensify social conflict and inequality and invariably affect the poorest, most socially, economically, environmentally and politically disadvantaged and vulnerable sectors of society'*. (The resolution needs to be read as a whole, but it is worth pointing out here the portions that signify major departures from standard UN positions.)

Taking account of the special needs of all those who have already been forced to leave their homes, the resolution places an injunction on governments to provide immediate resettlement with all the prerequisite services. It urges them to *'provide immediate restitution, compensation and/or appropriate and sufficient alternative accommodation or land, consistent with their wishes and needs, to persons and communities which have been forcibly evicted, following mutually satisfactory negotiations with the affected persons or groups'*.

The Sub-Commission on Human Rights

The UN body directly responsible for putting forward the resolution for action by the Commission is the Sub-Commission on Human Rights. In August 1991, the Sub-Commission adopted the first UN resolution on 'Forced Evictions'.[13] Taken together, the two resolutions form a significant departure from standard UN positions on such matters and constitute a powerful instrument for exposing the forces responsible for evictions. The Sub-Commission resolution, for example, admits that *'discrimination based on race, ethnic origin, nationality, gender, and social, economic and other status is often the actual motive behind forced evictions'*.

The role of policy making and planning is also exposed in the resolution, which states without reservation that *'misguided development policies can result in mass forced evictions'* and that *'governments often seek to disguise the violence that may be associated with forced evictions by using terms such as "cleaning the urban environ-ment", "urban renewal", "overcrowding" and "progress and development"'*.

The UN Committee on Economic, Social and Cultural Rights

The most relevant article of the ICESCR that has formed the basis for the Committee's work on Evictions and Housing Rights is Article 11(1): *'The States Parties to the present Covenant recognise the right of everyone to an adequate standard of living for himself and his family, including adequate food, clothing and housing and to the continuous improvement of living conditions'*. In its General Comment No.4, on the right to adequate housing, the Committee in a legal interpretation of Article 11(1) has explicitly stated that *'forced evictions are, prima facie, incompatible with the requirements of the ICESCR and could only be justified in the most exceptional circumstances and in accordance with the relevant principals of international law'*.[14]

In 1991 and 1992, the Committee, using evidence brought to its attention on evictions in Panama and the Dominican Republic, declared both these countries to be in violation of the Covenant.[15] The information that led to these historic pronouncements was made available by Habitat International Coalition, and the subsequent exposure which it achieved, combined with mobilisation work against the government policies in both these countries by local NGOs and mass-based campaigns, has led to a significant decrease in forced evictions.[16] The Committee continues to rebuke governments for forced evictions and to monitor the situation in the Philippines, Nicaragua, Kenya, Panama, and the Dominican Republic. Other countries that have received cautionary statements are Italy, Mexico, and Canada.[17]

The combined impact of the efforts described above, and in particular Habitat International Coalition's role in disseminating these pronouncements, has already resulted in the protection from planned evictions of at least 250,000 families, primarily in the countries of the Dominican Republic and Zambia.[18]

NGOs which have taken advantage of these channels to publicise their causes internationally and to minimise the forces causing violations of the Housing and Land Rights, including forced evictions, are the Brazilian Movement in the Defence of Life, Brazil; COPADEBA (Committee for the Rights of the Barrio) and Ciudad Alternativa, Dominican Republic; Urban Poor Associates and Saligan, Philippines; Unione Inquilini, Italy; Centre for Equality Rights and Accommodation, Canada; Habitat Mexico and Casa y Cuidad, Mexico; ZWOSAG, Zambia; and CONADEHUPA (National Commission of Human Rights in Panama), Panama.[19]

Conclusion

We can be certain that, given current social and political priorities whereby people are evicted to meet the needs of ill-defined development models, most governments will not voluntarily follow the imperatives laid down in the UN pronouncements. If anything, the priorities of governments are tending in the opposite direction. To take just one example from the recent stands being taken by some Asian countries, a new justification captures the selectivity with which States treat development options and issues of human rights. These Asian States have recently stated that the State's exclusive right to development is more important than human rights considerations. This is an apparently contradictory but convenient assertion, which allows for the concealment of human rights violations. The message is clear: forced evictions and a host of other gross violations of human rights will continue to be tolerated.

Given such double standards, mass organisations, trade unions, and campaigns against evictions should use the human rights instruments protecting the right to housing, including the two powerful resolutions described above. A special task rests with progressive lawyers in relevant countries, who must utilise the resolution, along with the relevant articles of National Constitutions, and build up legal arguments and develop case law so that the practice of forced evictions can be challenged. The immediate task, given that governments will not publicise this resolution, is to bring it to the notice of authorities and bureaucrats at all levels of the government. The media, which have covered this historic development from the UN only very superficially, can also play a valuable role, both locally and internationally, in publicising the resolution.[20]

In addition to the continuous involvement of the Committee on Economic, Social and Cultural Rights as described above, the UN Secretary-General has compiled an analytical report on forced evictions, based on an analysis of international law and jurisprudence and the responses received from governments, relevant UN agencies, and NGOs and community-based organisations. The report contains powerful recommendations to the UN system and the World's Governments, including urging the Commission on Human Rights to consider appointing a UN Special Rapporteur on Forced Evictions.[21]

It is vital that all concerned and interested people should contribute, particularly with strategies to counter evictions, to the work going on at the UN. This would be entirely in line with the fact that these recent developments are part of a new consciousness that has seeped into the work of the UN, primarily influenced by the vocal participation of concerned NGOs, which have taken full advantage of the spaces available within the UN system for the benefit of the causes they have been championing all along. An important initiative remains to be taken by the NGOs whose work is in the field of civil and political rights. The mandates of these groups at local, national, and international levels need to include issues such as forced evictions. The indivisibility of human rights – always accepted by the people and communities struggling for justice, and stressed in Vienna at the World Conference on Human Rights – needs to be translated into action, and the conceptual barriers broken down. Pressure must be maintained on governments worldwide, so that the reprehensible and illegal practice of forced evictions and the forces that abet this process can be exposed and stopped.

Notes

1   In particular the work of the Commission on Human Rights, the Sub-Commission on the Prevention of Discrimination and the Protection of Minorities, the Committee on Economic, Social and Cultural Rights, the Committee on the Elimination of Racial Discrimination, and the Committee on the Rights of the Child.

2   See UN doc. no. E/CN.4/Sub.2/1991/17 (Second Progress Report prepared by Danilo Turk, Special Rapporteur on the Realization of Economic, Social and Cultural Rights), pp.18-19. Mr Turk's final recommendations, presented in

1992, called for the appointment of a UN Special Rapporteur on the subjects of Housing, Income Distribution, and Population Transfer. Partly as a result of this, such appointments are gradually taking place.

3 See UN doc. no. E/CN.4/Sub.2/1992/15 (Working Paper prepared by Justice Rajindar Sachar on the Realisation of the Right to Adequate Housing).

4 See First Progress Report on the Right to Adequate Housing, prepared by the UN Special Rapporteur on the Right to Adequate Housing, August 1993, UN doc: E/CN.4/Sub.2/1993/15.

5 As of April 1993, the ICESCR has been ratified by 128 countries.

6 See 'General Comment No. 4 on the Right to Adequate Housing (Article11(1) of the Covenant on Economic, Social and Cultural Rights)', adopted by the Committee on Economic, Social and Cultural Rights on 12 December 1991 at its sixth session, UN doc: E/C.12/1991/4.

7 See in particular the line of reasoning developed by the UN Committee on Economic, Social and Cultural Rights in UN doc: E/C.12/1992/CRP.2/Add.3.

8 For an NGO-generated draft text of an Optional Protocol and for a discussion on the relevance of such an instrument, see the written submission to the UN World Conference on Human Rights, June 1993, by Food First International Network (FIAN) and Habitat International Coalition (HIC), 'Concerning an Optional Protocol to the Convention on Economic, Social and Cultural Rights', HIC, Mexico City, 1993.

9 See resolution titled 'Forced Evictions' (1993/77), adopted unanimously by the UN Commission on Human Rights on 10 March 1993.

10 See *A Global Survey of Forced Evictions: Violations of Human Rights*, (1994, 1993, 1992b 1992a, 1991, 1990), Habitat International Coalition, Mexico and the Centre on Housing Rights and Evictions; also see the written submissions on various aspects of housing rights and forced evictions by Habitat International Coalition to: (a) UN Commission on Human Rights (1988-1994); (b) UN Sub-Commission on Prevention of Discrimination and Protection of Minorities (1989-1993); and (c) UN Committee on Economic, Social and Cultural Rights (1988-1993).

11 See, for example, Walter Fernandes and Enakshi Thukral: *Development, Displacement and Rehabilitation: Issues for a National Debate*, Indian Social Institute, New Delhi, 1989.

12 For a discussion of how structural adjustment policies can lead to increased displacement, see National Campaign for Housing Rights: *Sapping India – Sapping the Indian People: The Impact of the IMF Structural Adjustment Package on Housing and Living Conditions in India*, NCHR, Bombay, 1992; also see Miloon Kothari and Ashish Kothari (1993): 'Structural adjustment vs. environment', *Economic and Political Weekly*, Vol. XXVIII no. 11, March, Bombay.

13 See resolution titled 'Forced Evictions' (1991/12), adopted unanimously by the UN Sub-Commission on the Prevention of Discrimination and the Protection of Minorities, 26 August 1991. For an analysis of this resolution, see Miloon Kothari and Scott Leckie (1992): 'United Nations condemns forced evictions', *Third World Resurgence*, no. 17, pp.43-5.

14 Op. cit., no. 6, UN doc. no. E/C.12/1991/4.

15 See UN docs. E/C.12/1990/B (p.64, Dominican Republic) and E/C.12/1991/4 (p.32 Panama), Reports of the Fifth and Sixth Sessions of the Committee on Economic, Social and Cultural Rights.

16 For examples of the kind of documentation that led to these pronouncements, see op. cit. no. 10(c); Habitat International Coalition (HIC) and CODEHUCA (1992): *Report on the Verification Visit of the Habitational Situation in Panama*, HIC, November 1992, Mexico City and Habitat International Coalition.

17 For the kind of documentation that has led the Committee to take action on countries, see Centre on Housing Rights and Evictions: '*Prima Facie* Violations of the Covenant on Economic, Social and Cultural Rights by the Government of Philippines' (November 1993); Urban Poor Associates, Saligan, *et al.*: *A Report to the United Nations Committee on Economic, Social and Cultural Rights on Housing Rights Abuses in the Republic of the Philippines 1986-1994*, Manila (April 1994); and Cuidad Alternativa: *Informe al Comité de los Derechos Economicos, Sociales y Culturales de ONU Sobre la Situación de los Desalojos en Republica Dominicana*, Santo Domingo (May 1994).

18 For a compilation of the various instruments that have assisted efforts in different countries to halt evictions, see Centre on Housing Rights and Evictions (COHRE) (1993): *Forced Evictions and Human Rights: A Manual for Action*, COHRE, Utrecht, June.

19 For a description of how the UN system can be utilised, see Miloon Kothari: 'Tijuca Lagoon; evictions and human rights in Rio de Janeiro', *Environment and Urbanisation*, vol. 6, No. 1, April 1994, International Institute of Environment and Development, London.

20 For a listing of options available to local and international groups to mobilise different sectors of society and the international community, see op. cit. no.17, Chapter 4.

21 See UN Secretary-General, Forced Evictions: Analytical Report Compiled by the Secretary-General submitted Pursuant to Commission on Human Rights Resolution 1993/77 (10 March 1993) UN doc. no. E/CN.4/1994/20. For a discussion on the relevance of the appointment of a UN Special Rapporteur on Forced Evictions, see op. cit. no. 18, Chapter 9.

The author

Miloon Kothari is a human rights activist involved since 1987 in research, advocacy, and networking on the issues of housing rights and forced evictions. Since 1991 he has represented the Habitat International Coalition (HIC, based in Mexico City) at the UN Human Rights bodies in Geneva. He is currently the Convener of the HIC Housing Rights Sub-Committee, responsible for HIC's Global Campaign on the Right to Housing, and its Global Campaign against Forced Evictions. He is a founding member and Co-Director of the Centre on Housing Rights and Evictions (COHRE), an advocacy group on economic, social, and cultural rights based in Utrecht, Netherlands. In these capacities he is currently working closely with community groups and campaigns on housing rights and against forced evictions in India, Palestine, Israel, Brazil, and Turkey to promote the housing-rights approach and to apply international human rights law in local and national situations.

This article was first published in *Development in Practice* Volume 5, Number 1 (1995).

Assisting survivors of war and atrocity:
notes of 'psycho-social' issues for NGO workers

Derek Summerfield

Introduction

What has been generally labelled the 'psycho-social' dimension of the impact of war and organised violence has been of increasing interest in the development field, and in agencies like the World Health Organisation (WHO) and United Nations High Commissioner for Refugees (UNHCR). This offers some positive possibilities, but the danger is that a narrowly 'medicalised' and 'psychologised' view of 'trauma' will be imposed in diverse settings worldwide. This would constitute a typical North–South transfer of concepts and practices.

Because this issue has become fashionable, funding is being attracted to some highly flawed proposals. What are the issues for agencies which aim first and foremost for the fullest possible understanding of the experiences of war-affected peoples and of the factors which shape their responses over time, including the decision to seek help? Can such NGOs enrich the relationships they forge with those they seek to assist, and go on to highlight new possibilities for well-grounded interventions?

The following notes are not intended to be prescriptive, but to sketch out a framework to guide workers in whatever war-affected setting they are addressing. Actual approaches and solutions have to be locally tailored.

1 There is a set of themes running through most modern conflict. Violence is played out where people live and work; there is little distinction between combatants and others; and more than 90 per cent of all casualties are civilian. Exemplary brutality is often systematically used to create terror as a means of control of whole populations. Abductions, extrajudicial executions, and torture are frequently public and witnessed by families of victims. Sexual violation is a standard and underreported element: women are exposed to this in prisons, in their homes in conflict zones, during flight, and in refugee camps. In twenty violent conflicts during the 1980s, children were not just passive bystanders, but also had active roles, including bearing arms — either as volunteers or through coercion. Damage, frequently intentional, to social, economic, and cultural institutions and ways of life takes place almost invariably. This may disrupt the way a particular people connect with their history, identity, and lived values, all of which define their world. Prominent and respected people — community leaders, health workers, priests, educated people — are often targeted. The neutrality of medical facilities is not respected.

The cumulative effect can mean that large numbers of civilians are rendered near-destitute, whether or not displaced from their communities. Modern conflict is frequently chronic and fluctuating, with hostilities varying in intensity and location. People feel besieged and threatened, even when their particular locality is quiet. Staying silent about what they have endured or seen may be important for survival. In many parts of the world, social tension and war are not extraordinary or 'abnormal'; their effects are so chronic that they have come to be incorporated into economic and social life; various groups, affected in varying ways, respond and adapt to the situation by diverse and shifting means.

2 Thus survivors suffer multiple injuries, not just to life and limb but to the social fabric of their communities, which may no longer be able to play its customary protective and problem-solving role. They will be horrified and grieving, not just for what has happened to individual human beings, but to their community, society, and culture. Most will register the wounds of war in social rather than psychological terms. Those who are refugees must also contend with the insecurities and hardship of their new situation, including (for some) a cultural gulf between themselves and the host society.

3 Fundamental to the human processing of atrocious experience is the subjective meaning it has or comes to have for those affected, the understandings and attributions they draw on in the struggle to encompass what has happened. These understandings, and the adaptations that flow from them, are drawn from society, its history and politics. People who have not been able to generate an interpretation of what has happened, and who find events incomprehensible, are likely to feel the most helpless and unsure what to do.

Help-seeking behaviour will be determined by background, culture, and social norms. War-affected communities are heterogeneous, and there will not be one standard reaction to events. Those affected are not 'pure' victims, and even the most destitute still exercise active interpretations and choices. They are victims, but they are also survivors. It is important to know as much as possible about how the particular society functioned in the past.

4 The sense which people make of their predicament, and the priorities they nominate, are not static; they may shift with time, with change in the war situation, and as people adapt and reorganise.

5 Supportive interventions for war-affected people must ideally be based upon an accurate and comprehensive grasp of the complexities of what has happened. Naturally this starts with appraisal of the scale and nature of the material damage and upheaval which the war has wrought. But the experience of people on the ground also involves subjective, less material elements. War provokes states of feeling and thinking which to the people concerned are not necessarily any less 'real' as reflections of what has happened than, say, the total numbers of dead and injured. For them this is part of the story of the war and is destined to become part of social memory. These factors will influence what survivors say and do, and what they want, and thus shape short-term and, arguably, longer-term outcomes for individuals and for their society.

6 NGO workers must be aware of these issues, and pay attention to the ways in which they may be manifesting themselves in a particular setting, if they are to deepen their background knowledge and capacity for accurate empathy with those they seek to assist. This may generate new possibilities for creative intervention and provide more criteria for choosing between proposed projects. It may minimise misunderstandings, make survivors feel more understood, and thus improve the relationship between NGO and 'client' group, whether the project is to do with emergency aid, agriculture, education, or whatever. Thus we are talking about *an approach*, about the way NGO workers engage with war-affected peoples, and not just about defined projects. The effectiveness of project evaluation will also be strongly influenced by the quality of this relationship over time.

7 NGO workers need first to reflect on their own assumptions about the personal impact of war, atrocity, torture and so on. Do you think, for example, that someone who has been tortured is likely to be psychologically disturbed or damaged, if not overtly, then under the surface? Psychological concepts are part of Western culture and thought and are thus not absolute or universal, though they are being increasingly globalised. 'Trauma', and a presumed need for psychological treatment, is a fashionable concept in the West and there is a danger of inappropriately applying it to war settings worldwide. Every culture has its own con-structions of traumatic events and recipes for recovery. Interventions aimed at alleviating the psychological distress of war-affected peoples may be simplistic and ignorant of local culture, and risk being experienced as insensitive or imposed. If this is so, they will fail anyway. Local workers can also feel undermined by imported concepts and 'experts' who implement them.

8 Wars cause distress or suffering, and this is of course understandable and 'normal'. We should not generally interpret and re-label this as psychological 'trauma', denoting a mental injury, analogous to a physical injury, needing treatment or 'therapy'. This basic error is already being made, at the risk of distortion in the wider debate about the effects of war and the prioritisation of resources to address them. Only a small minority develop a psychological problem which (if facilities permit) merits professional help. Expressions of distress, even when forceful, do not generally imply psychological frailty or damage, or nearness to breakdown. Survivors do not want to be psychologised or have some kind of 'sick' identity imputed to them. The few who do develop objective psychological disturbance generally show themselves by their inability to function properly in their situation. For this reason their family or community tend to identify them for themselves. It is not these few but the majority, and the processes which can sustain them, which will be the focus of interventions by the NGO field.

9 The narratives of survivors can give a graphic illustration of their experiences, what they mean to them, and the coping processes brought to bear on them. Some may seek to tell their stories to others, including NGO workers, to obtain ordinary human comfort and solidarity. However, we must not assume that this is what survivors *should* do if they want to get better; some cultures do not prescribe this, and even in the West individual needs vary.

10 What is fundamental is that suffering is a social experience and not a private one. What this suffering provokes in war-affected peoples is played out in public. They struggle to come to terms with their losses (which sometimes seem to amount to their whole world), engaging with their situation in what one hopes is a problem-solving way.

11 Provision of the essentials for daily living, and issues of physical security, obviously come first. Beyond that, the major thrust of NGO interventions will be towards the social world of survivor populations, for herein lie the sources of resilience and capacity for recovery for all. Thus the 'psycho-social' agenda is substantially a social one. Because of its association with the mental-health field, it might be better to drop the term 'psycho-social' in favour of one indicating that the core task is to address the social and collective wounds of war. *Interventions should not use a (mental) aid-and-relief model, addressing 'psychology', but a social development model, addressing suffering.*

12 Most people endure war and recover from it as a function of the extent to which they can, firstly, regain a measure of dignity, control, and autonomy over their immediate environment. They will seek to reconstitute what they can of their family and other networks, so often splintered in modern conflict. Anything that generates a sense of solidarity or community, and bolsters the viability of local organisations and structures, must be helpful. Meaningful training and work can be one logical focus of NGO efforts, allowing people to feel useful and effective again, as well as perhaps generating income or essential items for subsistence. Most people would rather be active citizens than mere recipients of aid. Involvement in projects can help people to sustain their weakened social relationships, or develop some new ones. In a partial way, such engagement can perform some of the functions which peacetime society used to do: helping people to generate a social meaning for events, to recognise, contain, and manage grief and its social face, mourning; to stimulate and organise active means of coping and problem-solving, individual and collective, in the face of continuing adversity.

And when in due course they get the chance, people will seek a substantial reconstruction of the damaged social fabric, including the economic and cultural forms and institutions which make sense to them. The restoration of health services and schooling are generally high priorities in all cultures. However, they will not necessarily seek just to restore to their old state what they valued before the war; they recognise that some things may have changed for ever.

13 NGO workers may represent a source of emotional support to war-affected people; but this is not, and does not have to be, 'therapy' or 'counselling', implying a professional activity with a technology. None the less, in some situations workers may feel empowered by some basic and contextualised advice on mental-health issues, either through contact with local professionals or from written material. An example of the latter are the succinct Save the Children Fund manuals on assisting children in difficult circumstances, notably war zones.

14 Those refugee camps which emphasise confinement and control, which provide residents with insufficient protection against further violence and abuse (often from within), or which do not involve them in decision-making obviously breach the basic principles outlined above. In some situations, NGOs also need to take account of the local people among whom refugees have come to rest. A good working relationship between them and the refugees may help both parties.

15 Much modern conflict worldwide is endemic, so that those affected have not even got to the stage of an aftermath and must keep up a kind of crisis-management response.

NGOs need to support the structures which help these people to endure and keep going. A proper counting of the costs and a 'recovery' have to be postponed.

16 There are few prescriptions which can be carried from one context to another: solutions need to be local, trading on survivors' resilience, skills, and priorities. War-affected peoples are often in fluid or evolving situations: with time, their perceptions and priorities may change, so their relationship with an NGO needs to be able to accommodate this. Will the NGO be able to detect and respond to such shifts, to join in their exploration of what is possible over time, without sacrificing clarity and rational planning?

17 While many of the experiences which war brings are shared by young men, young women and mothers, children and elderly alike, we may also delineate differential effects in some circumstances. For example, the key role of women, both in relation to their increased vulnerability (particularly to sexual and other violence) and their responsibilities as providers and protectors of the children, should be recognised. They often constitute the majority of adult refugees. Time needs to be taken to establish the expressed needs of women, both in their own right and in respect of those they care for.

Women can be the focus of projects which generate community-wide benefits. The physical and emotional well-being of children in war is strongly dependent on the capacity of their principal care-givers to cope. Once this fails, their morbidity and mortality rapidly escalate. Orphaned and otherwise unprotected children are a high-priority group and urgently need reconnecting, if possible, with surviving family members or others from their original community. All children need as much day-to-day normality and structure as can be managed, inside the home and outside it — for example, through the restoration of some schooling. People with physical disability (frequently war-induced) represent another group which may have distinct problems.

18 When we are discussing 'targeting', we should also note that there have been projects which focused exclusively either on a particular event such as 'rape', or a particular group, such as 'traumatised children', and so imposed a simplistic and decontextualised view of the experiences of survivors.

19 Some survivors are aware that their experiences amount to testimony which may have a wider political and legal significance, and are a part of the history of the war and a counting of its costs. It may apply universally that victims suffer more over time when they are denied official acknowledgement or reparation for what has been done to them. NGOs could consider collation, publication, and dissemination of their testimonies. This is evidence which could be presented to war-crimes tribunals and other forums.

20 To summarise, it is pivotal to recognise that the social fabric is a core target of modern warfare and in its damaged state remains the context in which large numbers of people must manage their distress and cope with their fractured lives. A basic task is to help them to sustain some social 'space' within which they can foster their collective capacities for endurance and creative survival.

The NGO field should largely avoid Western approaches which presuppose the incidence of mental trauma and tend to take a simplistic view of the complex and evolving experiences of war-affected populations. Too often, such approaches ignore the way in which people's experiences are shaped by their background norms and current understandings; and too often such approaches merely assign people the role of client or patient. Instead, the basic framework should adopt the model of social development — a model which is already well understood by the NGO field. Actual projects should ideally be locally tailored, situation-sensitive, able to adjust as circumstances change, and capable of taking root and thus of being self-sustaining.

The author

Derek Summerfield is a medical doctor with first-hand experience of war in Central America, Southern Africa and, via political refugees with a history of torture, in London. He has been a consultant to Oxfam (UK and Ireland) since 1990. He is currently principal psychiatrist at the Medical Foundation for the Care of Victims of Torture, London, and is a research associate at the Refugee Studies Programme, Queen Elizabeth House, Oxford.

This article was originally published in *Development in Practice*, Volume 5, Number 4 (1995).

Supporting education in emergencies:
a case study from southern Sudan

Alison Joyner

Permanent emergencies and the scope for development

'Emergencies' — war, famine, and natural disasters — create immediate basic needs. Shelter, water, food, and health and sanitation facilities are generally the priorities, particularly when there have been large-scale movements of population. Insecurity, political tensions, and fear often compound difficult physical conditions.

Is there time to consider the importance of education in such situations? The answer should be an unequivocal 'yes'. Education should be a crucial part of relief operations in emergencies. In practice, however, educational needs in emergencies have been neglected in competition with the demand for more conventional relief.

An example from southern Sudan demonstrates how educational needs can be addressed in an emergency. Indigenous initiatives for re-establishing and improving educational provision have been supported by a group of agencies working as part of the emergency operation. A flexible system of teacher education is the focus of a programme which invests in people rather than buildings. It emphasises the crucial importance of the involvement of local communities, on whom the success of rural primary school education depends.

Most relief operations are today dealing with areas in conflict. The list includes Rwanda, Bosnia, Angola, Liberia, Somalia, and others, besides Sudan. These 'complex emergencies' are becoming permanent, not a temporary interruption of a process of development soon to be restored.[1]

'Development', in the sense of longer-term change, is irrevocably affected by such emergencies. Violence and insecurity become part of the way of life. People often have to move, perhaps several times, to try to avoid conflict. Some form of 'normality' is re-established within the context of the upheaval.

The society affected continues to develop through the crisis. In this way, crisis itself can create opportunities as well as problems. The way in which the emergency is addressed must take into account these long-term implications. Education is a critical aspect of this approach.

The case of southern Sudan

The 'emergency' in southern Sudan started in 1983. The civil war — between the predominantly Muslim, Arab leadership in the north and a Christian/animist, African south — has destroyed the limited social services and infrastructure which previously existed. Hundreds of thousands of people have been displaced. Family and social structures have been severely disrupted.

The lack of educational facilities has serious consequences for relief operations. It is increasingly hard, for example, to find people with a sufficient level of school education to be trained as health workers. The implications of this, both now and for the future, are severe, however the war develops.

Schools began again to be set up in areas held by the SPLA (Sudan People's Liberation Army) in southern Sudan in 1988. Many were in rural areas, where there had never previously been a school: a positive step, prompted by the emergency. The schools are run and supported by local communities under the guidance of the relief wings of the two factions of the SPLA: the Sudan Relief and Rehabilitation Association (SRRA) and the Relief Association of South Sudan (RASS). An estimated 900 schools are operating in these areas.

The teachers in these schools are unpaid. A few are well qualified and experienced. Most have had only a few years' schooling and no teacher training. Many schools operate under trees. Any school buildings are usually built from local materials. There are some dilapidated permanent structures left from earlier government and NGO inputs, but no means to repair them. There are almost no textbooks, and basic school materials are inadequate.

Girls are a very small proportion of those children who do go to school. Estimates suggest that girls represent between one and ten per cent of the majority of school rolls. Cultural factors work strongly against rapid change in this situation.

Support for existing structures

Limited support was offered to schools in some areas up to 1993. Materials and a little training were provided by individual NGOs and UNICEF. As an 'emergency relief' operation, Operation Lifeline Sudan (OLS, a consortium of agencies operating in Sudan under a UN umbrella) was slow to recognise the place of education within its sphere of activity.

The Education Coordination Committee (ECC) of OLS (southern sector) was established in February 1993. It comprises representatives from RASS and SRRA, NGOs, organisations such as churches involved in education, and UNICEF.

The ECC aims to consolidate education work throughout SPLA-held areas of southern Sudan. It seeks to support the education structures already existing under the auspices of RASS and SRRA. Its success rests on the willingness of all parties to cooperate towards improving the quality of school education available to children in southern Sudan.

Establishing priorities

The ECC provides a forum for discussion between those locally responsible for the existing system — represented by SRRA and RASS — and those willing to support them. A sense of direction and priorities has evolved, and teacher education has been identified as the key activity, based on some fundamental principles:

• The educational level of most teachers needs up-grading, alongside professional training. This is recognised in the concept of *teacher education*, rather than *teacher training* alone.

• Improved education and training is an investment in people which can survive physical destruction. Teachers trained in earlier schemes re-emerge sometimes hundreds of miles from where they trained.

• To improve the quality of education in school, competent teachers are essential.

• Teachers are respected members of their community. Raising their awareness of the importance of such issues as health, girls' education, and psycho-social needs is a crucial first step to long-term and culturally appropriate development in these fields.

In-service teacher education

To implement teacher education in the context of a war, flexibility and mobility are essential. If an area becomes unstable, the population will move, and agencies pull out. Resources must be moveable too.

Training materials
The ECC is developing a modular teacher-education scheme at five levels. Each level involves a two-to-three week in-service course held inside Sudan, covering academic and professional subjects.

Materials for distance education are being written by educationists who are either southern Sudanese or have extensive experience of southern Sudan. Materials are designed for continued use as a reference after intensive, limited contact time with tutors on the in-service courses.

Textbooks in English and local languages are supplied to support the teacher-education courses.[2] Training is given in how to use the books as part of the course modules.

Training of trainers

The long-term aim is to train enough southern Sudanese trainers to run courses without expatriate personnel. This will take time, as the number of southern Sudanese teachers able to work as trainers is currently very small. Meanwhile, trainers are NGO staff or are seconded from the teaching profession in Kenya and Uganda.

A number of international NGOs have southern Sudanese staff members. These people are crucially important as a link with local people and in helping to evaluate the appropriacy of the courses and their future direction.

A workshop facilitated by the ECC was held before the first courses, to introduce 60 senior teachers and education coordinators to the course materials and textbooks. These people are now involved in their areas in helping to run the in-service courses. They are also responsible for following up and supporting the teachers who attend the courses after they return to their schools.[3]

The psycho-social importance of schools in a war zone

The psychological importance of schools in the context of war is considerable, particularly among displaced populations. Schools are symbolic of a return to some form of recognisable routine. They are often among the first community structures to be re-established during or after disruption caused by war.

Psycho-social needs have received increased attention in recent years. Schools provide the ideal forum for reaching, through teachers, war-affected children and adults. Teacher-education courses include a discussion module to raise awareness of psycho-social needs. More advanced training for teachers has been run in some areas, and it is planned to expand this.

Community support for schools

The key to the support of schools rests with local communities. Schools were initially established at the village level, with local people who volunteer their time for whatever payment in kind the community can give — frequently nothing. Where there are school buildings, they are often built by villagers. Parent Teacher Councils and village elders generally oversee such involvement.

No material support is available from the civilian administration for education. The limited funds available to outside agencies are best concentrated on providing resources such as training which cannot be found within Sudan. The day-to-day running of schools will be threatened if it is dependent on the inevitably precarious support of agencies operating in a 'relief' context.

Agencies of the ECC have sought ways of helping to stimulate community support. Items which complement the community input have been provided, such as seeds and tools for school gardens (600 in 1993 and 1994). The aim is to enable schools to produce vegetables which can be used to support teachers or children. The school garden should also be used as an educational experience for the pupils. Another form of input is the provision of sewing materials for women's tailoring groups to make school clothes.

Women's tailoring groups have been supplied with cloth and sewing materials in several pilot areas. A proportion of the cloth (normally two thirds) is used to make school clothes for pupils and teachers, prioritising dresses for girls. Recipients barter for the clothes, which provides a small income for the school. The remaining cloth is payment for the women. UNICEF supplies more cloth on receipt of forms to show that the clothes have been made and received by the school.

Basic education materials in the form of Education Kits are also supplied to all schools by UNICEF. The contents of the kits (currently being revised) are chalk, exercise books, pens and pencils, and a football. None of these can be purchased in southern Sudan.

Looking to the future: key issues

What has been achieved so far in southern Sudan is only a beginning. Within the structure of teacher education which has been established, a number of issues need to be considered as the system develops.

Quality of school education

The impact of improvements in the provision of school education must be measured in terms of *quality* and *appropriateness* to southern Sudan. School education should help to provide *life skills* useful in a rural context where the majority of children cannot expect more than a few years' primary education. Existing materials and methods will need to be revised in the light of experience of the teacher-education courses, and extensive follow-up and involvement with communities.

Certification/assessment

Assessment and certificates provide important recognition for teacher trainees and pupils, but should also reflect achievement that is relevant to their holders.

School examinations need to be compared with systems in neighbouring countries and as far as possible made compatible with them. The few pupils who are able to continue beyond primary education will have to do so outside Sudan for the foreseeable future.

External moderation is a priority for both school and teacher-education examinations.

Access

The imbalance between the number of girls and boys in school needs urgent attention. Understanding the cultural factors which affect the attendance of girls is essential. Only by working with communities to establish why education for girls is important will change gradually come about.

Ways of improving access for all children need to be found, within the constraints imposed by the shortage of teachers and other resources. Supporting local education coordinators in planning for this process — which is already clear as an issue for them — is an important role for staff of NGOs and other agencies working in southern Sudan.

When a school receives attention — education materials or training for teachers — the number of children attending invariably rises. As rural communities are convinced of improved quality and access, school attendance rates will improve.

Conclusion

The experience of southern Sudan has provided valuable lessons for other situations of conflict. It has shown that education is both an essential and a possible component of emergency operations.

The key elements of the programme can be summed up as follows.

- Focusing on people more than buildings through teacher education.
- Building on the existing involvement of communities to support school education.
- Fostering cooperation and consistency of approach between agencies.
- Recognising the importance of schools for conveying information and stimulating discussion on topics such as health, psycho-social needs, and girls' education, and integrating these cross-cutting issues into teacher education.
- Advocating to donors the importance of funding for education as a part of emergency operations.

Notes

1 Mark Duffield, 'Complex emergencies and the crisis of developmentalism', *IDS Bulletin: Linking Relief and Development*, Vol. 25, No. 3, October 1994.

2 English was chosen by the SPLA as the medium of instruction for schools in their areas. It has been agreed through discussions in the ECC that books produced by the Sudan Literature Centre (SLC) can be supplied to schools. SLC is run by southern Sudanese educationists producing trial editions of textbooks in English for the first five or six years of primary education, depending on subject. They are based on a syllabus designed for southern Sudan under a pre-war regional Ministry of Education.

3 Follow-up visits are made to schools to support and offer advice to the recent trainees, and to assess the impact of courses on teachers and schools. NGO staff support RASS and SRA Education Coordinators to do this in their areas. A supervision form has been agreed by the ECC, to give consistency and means of comparison between schools and areas in the formal assessments.

The author

Alison Joyner was from 1992 to 1994 the Project Officer for Education for UNICEF/ Operation Lifeline Sudan (southern sector), before which she was a teacher at the Sudan University for Science and Technology in Khartoum. She later became SCF (UK) Education Project Manager in the South Sudan Programme. She is currently Education Adviser for SCF in Lhasa, Tibet.

This article was originally published in *Development in Practice*, Volume 6, Number 1 (1996).

Family tracing: in whose interests?[1]

Lucy Bonnerjea

'He does not know the names of his ancestors; she does not know how to shop or cook or look after babies; none of them fits into society any more. This is what our institutions have done.'

Family tracing

In every war, disaster, or population displacement, children become separated from their families. Often they are lost when they flee from attacks on villages or when they are travelling long distances looking for food or safety. Some are kidnapped, abducted, or abandoned.

Past responses have often been to keep these children together. Most governments and NGOs have placed children in orphanages, in children's sections of refugee or transit camps, even deliberately separating them for feeding in camps or hospitals. This has generally been done for the best of motives: children come first, they are the most vulnerable, they need priority attention. The main concern has been their immediate safety and survival.

Family-tracing projects, however, argue that, in most cases, members of these children's families can be found, and living with them is in their best interests. Families are thought to be best for the child's development, protection, and long-term sense of identity. They are the place where social skills are learned, where members share the same language and the same culture, and where there is a shared ancestry. Children learn how families work, how roles are developed, because they have social and economic models to observe and from which to learn. This gives a sense of continuity: a past that people know about, which links to the future.[2]

Can it be done?

Can families be traced in the middle of a war or drought? Not always, but often they can — depending largely on how good a tracing programme exists. Such a programme entails bringing together clearly developed principles and values (on the importance of children having families, and communities having their children back) as well as efficient logistics and systems, including excellent record keeping, filing systems, and good transport.

Family tracing is usually tackled in four stages: identifying the children who need tracing; documenting information from them; tracing family members; and, where possible, reuniting children with their families. Gender-determined differences must be considered at every stage, since the circumstances and experiences of boys and girls often vary considerably.

Identification

Identifying the children who need assistance is the first step. Children cannot be expected to ask for tracing; they must be offered it. Some programmes begin with the visibly separated children, such as those in a children's feeding centre or children's home. Others systematically map the places where separated children may be found (in police stations, in the streets, in the community) and decide which children are the most vulnerable, and which need a tracing service first.

Identifying the children often needs a national education programme. Wars usually create a great deal of fear and mistrust about the abuse of personal information. People fear being victimised, punished, abducted — for who they are, and not for what they have done. They will volunteer personal information only if they understand and accept the tracing programme.

Documentation

Documenting children is the next step. It involves getting information from individual children about the past, the present, and their wishes for the future. There are many obstacles to adults listening to and hearing children. All over the world, children are expected to listen to adults, rather than the other way round: this makes listening to children a skill that has to be taught and developed in a family-tracing programme. Some children may not know their family name or the name of their village. Some may be too traumatised to remember.

Documentation depends on building a trusting relationship, encouraging each child to talk, and then recording all bits of information. Some children, especially the older ones, will be able to provide factual information from which a tracing trip can be planned. Others will need to be asked questions such as: were there any rivers near where you lived, any mountains, any schools? Where did you buy bread? Did the shopkeeper know you? Was there a church or mosque or market?

Having got the facts, there are two more sets of questions. The first is about the child's short-term needs: is she safe and happy staying where she is, while the tracing takes place? Or should she be moved to somewhere safer or better? The second is about her long-term needs, such as which relatives would she like to live with? This is usually relevant only if parents are dead or not found; then the choice of alternative family members needs to be made with the child.

Tracing

Tracing means going off into the unknown, often over-land, and covering long distances on foot. It means asking at market places, meeting village elders and local leaders, sometimes carrying photographs of the children, sometimes taking only the documentation forms, sometimes together with the children themselves. Tracing may also be done through newspapers, posters, or radio.

Tracing works only if it is done with the help of people living in the areas from which the children come. It relies on information from communities; it needs people to place their trust in the tracing staff, to discuss possibilities, and to identify neighbours, relatives, or local leaders who might help. Tracing works best through recognised local leadership structures, whether traditional or religious leaders, elders, or chiefs.

Reunification

Reunification is the goal. Ideally, family members are found, the children want to live with them, and the family is happy to have them. But it is important to assess whether there is enough food to feed the child, and whether the area is reasonably secure. Then the child can be returned, often with dancing, music, and thanks to the ancestors.

Often the reality is more difficult, and tracing staff face a great many problems before anyone is located. They might find that parents and grandparents are definitely or probably dead. Other family members may be very distantly related and economically destitute. What does one do? Each family situation needs to be assessed, with recognised authorities within the community invited to discuss whether families can and should look after the child. Limited economic help may be offered.

Substitute families may be needed, either as a short-term placement, while the search for families continues; or as a long-term placement, when avenues for searching have been exhausted. Again, local help is needed, to assess the families' motivation and economic situation. Monitoring remains important, whether this is done by social workers, community leaders, or adults chosen by the child.

In whose interest?

But one must always ask in whose interest it is to conduct a family-tracing programme or an individual placement. Each programme planner, funder, and evaluator, as well as each member of the tracing team, needs to ask this question constantly, as a reminder of the goals of family tracing. This should not only be about closing feeding programmes, saving money on institutional care, or following new fashions in NGO project design. Nor should it be about dumping children at the first available opportunity in any community setting. The long-term interests of the children — in the context of their culture, their language, their safety, their development, and their countries — must be considered, together with their short-term survival. We have now come full circle.

We used to take children out of their communities, 'in their own interests'. We are now returning them to their own communities, again 'in their own interests'. We need to open up the debate about what really is in the child's own interests, in each country, in each emergency, and in each development situation.

Notes

1 This article is based on a review of SCF's programmes in five African countries: Angola, Ethiopia, Liberia, Mozambique, and Uganda. Some are operational projects, others consist of funding and supporting national government staff to do the work. In each case, the review consisted in examining the programme and interviewing government policy-makers, community-based tracing staff, SCF staff, families, and children. In addition, two pieces of research were commissioned: a postal survey of all social action staff in Mozambique who had carried out tracing and reunification of children, and a follow-up of 100 families in Uganda, where children had been returned after varying lengths of separation. Children and families were interviewed separately.

2 Families are synonymous neither with parents nor with household members. Family structures vary enormously. Extended families play very important roles, and in this context the family constitutes anyone to whom the child is related, by blood or marriage.

The author

Lucy Bonnerjea, a lecturer at the London School of Economics, was commissioned by Save the Children Fund to carry out a review of five family-tracing programmes. A guide to good practice, based on this work, was published by SCF in early 1994.

This article was originally published in *Development in Practice*, Volume 4, Number 3 (1994).

Annotated bibliography

This is a selective listing of recent English-language publications about development work in the context of crisis and armed conflict, with particular reference to Complex Humanitarian Emergencies (CHEs). Much of the richest and most innovative thinking in this field is to be found in unpublished programme evaluation reports, in scholarly journals, or in detailed case-studies. Here, we have focused on major works and material that is readily accessible; most of them also have bibliographies to which readers can refer. Country-specific material has been cited where it illustrates broader issues of humanitarian policy and practice, or where it gives voice to those directly affected by war and armed conflict. A listing of major international research projects is included; most of them publish studies in their own right, and hold specialised databases or documentation centres.

The Bibliography was compiled and annotated by Deborah Eade and Caroline Knowles, Editor and Reviews Editor respectively of Development in Practice, *with Stephen Commins and Chris Jackson.*

African Rights: *Humanitarianism Unbound? Current Dilemmas Facing Multi-mandate Relief Operations in Political Emergencies*
Discussion Paper No 5
London: African Rights, 1994
A study of the moral and practical dilemmas posed by the 'unbridled' involvement of NGOs in post-Cold War complex emergencies, and a fierce critique of their role in making influential (and often naive or opportunist) political judgements that are 'apparently unimpeded by limits on their mandate and expertise, or by accountability'. Examining the performance of NGOs and UN agencies in Ethiopia, Sudan, Angola, Somalia, Bosnia, and Rwanda, the authors call for NGOs to clarify their ethical mandate and operational principles and apply them in a clear and consistent manner.

Mary B Anderson and P J Woodrow: *Rising from the Ashes: Development Strategies in Times of Disaster*
Paris: UNESCO/Boulder: Westview Press, 1989

Building on several case-studies, the authors show that relief programmes are never neutral in their impact on development. They present a simple framework (known as CVA: Capacities and Vulnerabilities Analysis) for understanding the dynamic relationship between different people's needs, vulnerabilities, and capacities. Assessing current emergency-relief practice, the authors show various practical ways in which it might be improved.

Jon Bennett: *Meeting Needs: NGO Coordination in Practice*
London: Earthscan, 1995
A compilation of eight case-studies documenting examples of NGO coordination in emergencies in the Middle East, the Horn of Africa, Cambodia, and Central America. An overview examines the dangers of NGO expansion in emergencies, especially where it allows bilateral and multilateral aid to be channelled through the non-governmental sector at the expense of Southern governments and public-service structures. It asks why NGOs

coordinate best in crisis, and what their true impact is if they undermine government structures.

Michael Cranna (ed): *The True Cost of Conflict*
London: Earthscan with Saferworld, 1994
Since 1945, some 22 million people have died in wars, and many of the 42 million displaced persons worldwide are victims of conflict. This book assesses the true costs, using case-studies of the Gulf War, East Timor, Mozambique, Peru, Kashmir, Sudan, and former Yugoslavia. It examines the human casualties, as well as the consequences in social, developmental, and environmental terms. It also attempts to calculate the wider costs both to the countries involved and to their economic partners, and asks who ultimately benefits from conflict.

Ilene Cohn and Guy S Goodwin-Gill: *Child Soldiers: The Role of Children in Armed Conflict*
Oxford: Oxford University Press, 1994
War has caused the death of two million children and left six times as many without homes since the mid-1980s. Related to this is 'the increased participation of children in hostilities, in terms both of numbers and the ... nature of their involvement'. Written for the Henry Dunant Institute of the Red Cross, this book examines the plight of child soldiers in the context of International Humanitarian Law (IHL) and the 1989 Convention on the Rights of the Child. Drawing on data from Africa, Asia, and Latin America, the authors explore the motivations of child soldiers, as well as those of the adults who recruit and exploit them.

Mark Cutts and A Dingle: *Safety First: Protecting NGO Employees who Work in Areas of Conflict*
London: Save the Children Fund, 1995
Humanitarian organisations which work in war zones must weigh their responsibility to the affected populations against their obligation to protect their own employees. This book advises NGOs on how they can better protect

their staff, and so improve their chances of continuing their humanitarian work. Drawing on SCF's experience, it examines safety in terms of basic principles such as risk management and non-partisanship; safety-conscious management practices; and practical security measures. It also offers advice on the evacuation of employees, and explaining actions to the media.

Mark Duffield: 'Complex emergencies and the crisis of developmentalism', *IDS Bulletin*, 25/4: 37-45, October 1994
In this influential paper, the author draws a direct relationship between political instability and the rise of internal wars and complex political emergencies, which threaten to destroy the entire cultural, civil, political, and economic integrity of a society. Ethnic factors are common to these emergencies. Relief agencies and NGOs often fail to recognise the distinction between natural disasters and complex emergencies, and so adopt 'linear' analyses and responses based on inappropriate assumptions about the possibility of 'a return to normal'. Instead, they should design their programmes around the fact that complex emergencies are the norm in the post-Cold War era. However, in shaping their appeals (and hence their accountability) to their donors rather than to those affected by political violence, NGOs may implicitly further Western disengagement from a commitment to equitable development.

Deborah Eade and Suzanne Williams: *The Oxfam Handbook of Development and Relief*
Oxford: Oxfam Publications, 1995
This three-volume reference book offers an authoritative guide to policy and practice in every area of development and emergency-relief work in which Oxfam is involved. Chapter Two, 'Focusing on People', explores those aspects of social identity that should inform all development and emergency relief work, such as gender, ethnic and cultural identity, childhood, old age, and disability. Chapter Six, 'Emergencies and Development', focuses largely on Complex Humanitarian

Emergencies involving war and armed conflict. Oxfam's accent is on building sustainable local capacities both to identify needs and deliver assistance, and also to reduce vulnerability in the longer term. Detailed sections address practical issues concerning NGO coordination, needs assessment, nutrition, environmental health (including water, sanitation, and housing), and food security. Each section includes Key Questions and Further Resources. A 500-entry annotated *NGO Resources Directory* comprises the third volume, and is also published separately.

Susan Forbes Martin: *Refugee Women*
London: Zed Books, 1992
Despite growing awareness of the disproportionate vulnerability of women in situations of conflict, and the so-called 'gender violence' of rape and sexual abuse, aid agencies still show a weak understanding of how to design relief interventions in a gender-sensitive way. Even agencies with gender policies may suggest that gender analysis is a unaffordable luxury in a crisis. The book examines five areas that are central to refugees' well-being: protection, access to social and material services, economic activity, repatriation and reconstruction, and resettlement in a third country. Straightforward and gender-sensitive policy and practice alternatives are presented for each area.

Ted Robert Gurr: *Minorities at Risk: A Global View of Ethnopolitical Conflicts*
Washington: United States Institute of Peace Press, 1993
Communal identity may be based on shared historical experiences or myths, religious beliefs, language, ethnicity, region of residence, and, in castè-like systems, customary occupations. The identification of what are often referred to as ethnic groups or minorities depends not on the presence of particular traits, but on the shared perception that these set the group apart. Surveying over 200 politically active communal groups, the author asks: what communal identities and interests are most at odds with the structures

and policies of existing states, and why? Strategies to reduce ethnic conflict, such as autonomy, pluralism, and formal power-sharing are discussed.

International Committee of the Red Cross: *Basic Rules of the Geneva Conventions and their Additional Protocols*
Geneva: ICRC, 1983
A booklet summarising the basic rules of International Humanitarian Law (IHL), which lays out agreements concerning the protection of the victims of armed conflicts, for which there are some 600 provisions in the Geneva Conventions and their Additional Protocols. Further information about IHL and details of other publications are available from ICRC (qv).

Michael T Klare and Daniel C Thomas (eds): *World Security: Challenges for a New Century*
New York: St Martin's Press (second edition), 1994
A collection of essays on the post-Cold War world, reflecting on how recent global changes will affect future world security. The first four focus on the broad political and social contours of the emerging international system. Others cover nuclear proliferation, arms trafficking, ethnic and regional conflict, Third World militarism, international human rights, violence against women, environmental degradation, demographic change, under-development, and hunger.

Mary Ann Larkin, Frederick C Cuny, Barry N Stein (eds): *Repatriation Under Conflict in Central America*
Georgetown: CIPRA and Intertect, 1991
As a result of the wars in Central America in the 1970s and 1980s, many rural (often indigenous) populations were displaced or became homeless. Most remained as internally displaced persons, with little access to international protection and assistance. Of the many thousands who sought asylum abroad, few acquired refugee status, but faced instead the fear and insecurity of being undocumented or

illegal migrants. Continued conflict seemed to render repatriation inconceivable. However, many refugees returned from the mid-1980s, firstly in a spontaneous movement, and later with assistance from UNHCR and others.

Worldwide, most displaced persons either do not qualify for, or do not have access to, international aid; and most refugees return home with little or no international assistance. In analysing specific cases of spontaneous and/or unassisted voluntary repatriation, the essays in this book illustrate the wider dilemmas of policy and practice which the phenomenon poses for humanitarian agencies.

A companion volume, *Repatriating During Conflict in Africa and Asia* (1992), also edited by Cuny *et al.*, is published by the Center for the Study of Societies in Crisis. For a summary of the main issues, see B N Stein and F K Cuny: 'Refugee repatriation during conflict: protection and post-return assistance', *Development in Practice*, 4/3: 173-87.

Mandy Macdonald and Mike Gatehouse: *In the Mountains of Morazan: Portrait of a Returned Refugee Community in El Salvador*
London: Latin America Bureau, 1995
An account of a Salvadoran community of 8,000, who returned in the midst of civil conflict after nine years as refugees in Honduras. The Ciudad Segundo Montes faced unanticipated problems in the transition to post-war reconstruction. With declining foreign aid and international concern, and without public investment or state subsidies, people had to abandon many of the beliefs and organisational approaches that had motivated and bound them while in exile. The book provides unique insights into experiences shared by poor people who struggle to rebuild their lives in a post-war (and post-Cold War) framework, and so move from survival and subsistence to development.

Joanna Macrae and Anthony Zwi (eds): *War and Hunger: Rethinking International Responses to Complex Emergencies*
London and New Jersey: Zed Books, 1994
A compilation of papers (with contributions by David Keen, Alex de Waal, Mark Duffield, and Hugo Slim) examining the relationships between poverty, armed conflict, food insecurity, and the dilemmas of providing humanitarian relief in times of war. Complex Humanitarian Emergencies are inherently political, whether they take the form of genocide (or 'ethnic cleansing') or other forms of human-rights violations (such as the denial of food to certain population groups). Donors and NGOs often fail to comprehend the underlying political causes; and the failures of international aid efforts are partly due to this. Drawing largely on case-studies from Africa, authors call for greater clarity and accountability in the international relief system, arguing that transitional (post-conflict) issues must be addressed by local organisational structures.

David Millwood (ed): *The International Response to Conflict and Genocide: Lessons from the Rwanda Experience*
Steering Committee of the Joint Evaluation of Emergency Assistance to Rwanda (5 volumes), available from Overseas Development Institute, UK, 1996
The Joint Evaluation of Emergency Assistance to Rwanda takes as its starting point the fact that the massive humanitarian operation engendered by the Rwandan crisis ought never to have been necessary in the first place. Had appropriate political and diplomatic action been taken at an earlier stage, much of the human devastation resulting from the genocide might have been prevented. The report, which comprises four separate studies and a synthesis document, examines the background of the 1994 crisis, the role of key international players, and the performance of the myriad organisations involved in humanitarian assistance and post-war reconstruction efforts. Few of those involved escape criticism: the report poses serious challenges for the UN General Secretariat, the Security Council, influential regional and OECD governments, the UN's humanitarian agencies and human rights machinery, NGOs, and the media. Important recommendations are made concerning the future management of such

interventions, and the report is likely to influence debate on 'complex emergencies' for some time to come.

Larry Minear and Thomas G Weiss: *Humanitarian Action in Times of War*
Boulder: Lynne Rienner Publishers, 1993
A handbook synthesising lessons and setting out humanitarian principles and policy guidelines for civilian actors involved in providing humanitarian assistance and protection in wars and other armed conflicts. Despite differences among them, UN organisations, donor governments, NGOs, ICRC, and institutions working in conflict areas all share a basic commitment to these principles.

Agencies that are clear and consistent in how they articulate and observe certain humanitarian principles are thought to function most successfully in situations of conflict. But when agencies rely on improvisation, unconstrained by fidelity to stated principles of action, they perform less adequately. A range of practical considerations is offered in the interests of improving performance and accountability, together with a proposed practitioners' code of conduct for humanitarian organisations, both individually and as a community.

Larry Minear and Thomas G Weiss: *Mercy Under Fire*
Boulder: Westview Press, 1995
Describing the experience of the international community in responding to the increase in violent conflict in the early post-Cold War period, the authors review efforts to provide assistance and protection to civilian populations. Writing for the concerned international public, the authors draw on many interviews with relief workers, and provide non-specialists with an insight into the challenges faced by humanitarian aid professionals.

Terence Loone Mooney (ed): *The Challenge of Development within Conflict Zones*
Paris: OECD, 1995
Three papers from a 1994 OECD Colloquium, with an overview and conclusion. Larry Minear sets out a conceptual framework for

discussing development in conflict. He analyses the responsibilities of, constraints on, and opportunities for donors, UN peace-support operations, and NGOs. Mary B Anderson looks at how the international community might provide political and moral help to societies emerging from conflict, in order to reduce tensions, support development, and build the wider conditions for sustainable peace. Kumar Rupesinghe discusses the relationship between conflict and development and calls for a 'strategic umbrella' approach to conflict-prevention, under which country-specific consortia of concerned government bodies and NGOs, co-operating with inter-governmental groups, would focus on addressing situations of emerging conflict.

Oxfam Working Papers include: *Development in Conflict: The Gender Dimension* (1994); *Conflict and Development: Organisational Adaptation in Conflict Situations* (1995); *The Somali Conflict: Prospects for Peace* (1994); *Famine, Needs Assessment, and Survival Strategies in Africa* (1993); and *War and Famine in Africa* (1991).

Jenny Pearce: *Promised Land: Peasant Rebellion in Chalatenango, El Salvador*
London: Latin America Bureau, 1986
A detailed and compelling account of grassroots development that took place in the guerrilla-held war zones of El Salvador, as defined and run by peasant communities in the area. Activities included education and adult literacy, community health work, agricultural production, and systems of community policing, as well as the organisational skills required to manage them.

Rosemarie Rogers and Emily Copeland: *Forced Migration: Policy Issues in the Post-Cold War World*
Medford, Massachussets: Tufts University, 1993
This book highlights the lack of international protection and assistance for internally displaced persons who have 'fled conditions of generalised violence in which their own

government is involved or which it cannot control'. It questions the conventional separation between internal and external affairs, where national sovereignty acts as a shield behind which a government allows sectors of its population to be forcibly displaced. The obligation to protect and promote human rights resides with States, and hence with the international community. Policies to assist refugees and displaced persons require that forced migration be addressed primarily as a major violation of human rights.

Shawn Roberts and Jody Williams: *After the Guns Fall Silent: The Enduring Legacy of Landmines*
Washington: Vietnam Veterans of America Foundation, 1995
Describing the effect of landmines on people, their communities, their lives and livelihoods, this book examines the consequences of landmine use on refugee movement and resettlement, and on the environment. It also covers issues such as mine clearance and mine-awareness, and medical, rehabilitative, and psychological costs.

Robert I Rotberg and Thomas G Weiss (eds): *From Massacres to Genocide: the Media, Public Policy and Humanitarian Crises*
Cambridge, MA: Brookings Institute/The World Peace Foundation, 1986
Discussion of the way that media coverage of international crises influences policy-making. Contributors all agree on the importance of well-informed and well-developed media attention for the formulation of sensible policies regarding the resolution of ethnic and religious conflict and complex humanitarian crises. The issue is examined from many angles: how the media cover emergency situations, and the influence of the media (particularly television) on both governmental decision-making and NGO actions; the views of humanitarian groups on the limitations of media coverage, especially how they can help the media maintain high standards when issues are reduced to sound bites; the current state of policy-making in the United States; and the disputed effects of media coverage and public opinion on policy formulation.

Kumar Rupesinghe (ed): *Ethnic Conflict and Human Rights*
Tokyo: UN University Press, 1994
Based on a 1986 seminar (sponsored by the UN University, International Alert, the Norwegian Human Rights Institute, and the International Peace Research Institute). Contributors explore ethnic conflicts and their relationship to human rights. Reviewing theories of ethnic conflict-resolution, and various historical, social, political, and legal factors, they seek elements of potential strategies for ending conflicts and promoting peace. The collection includes case-studies of Northern Ireland, South Africa, Nicaragua, and Sri Lanka.

Hugo Slim: 'The continuing metamorphosis of the humanitarian professional: some new colours for an endangered chameleon', *Disasters*, 19/2: 110-26 June 1995
Relief agencies now work in operational situations — complex humanitarian emergencies — that call for re-training (or re-skilling). This requires a fundamental reappraisal of what constitutes humanitarian work, which now includes political analysis, negotiation skills, conflict prediction and management, and information-gathering capacity. For NGOs, new demands include working with armed guards and/or military forces, specific country information (not relief generalities), involvement in community peace-building, and a better understanding of physical and mental health issues.

Rodolfo Stavenhagen: *The Ethnic Question: Conflicts, Development, and Human Rights*
Tokyo: UN University Press, 1990
A comprehensive picture of contemporary ethnic issues, as manifested in most of the world's major regions. After discussing such issues in relation to the theories of nation, State, modernisation, and class, the case of Latin America is analysed in depth. The author examines the extent of ethnic rights protection

in the UN and other international systems, the problems of indigenous and tribal peoples, racism in Western Europe, and government cultural and education policies in relation to ethnic minorities.

Anjali Sundaram and George Gelber (eds): *A Decade of War: El Salvador Confronts the Future*
London: CIIR (with Monthly Review Press and Transnational Institute), 1991
This collection of ten commissioned articles addresses three broad themes: the concept and practice of democracy in El Salvador; the Duarte period and the role of US political, economic, and military intervention; and major social forces within the country — the Church, the popular movement, political parties, the armed forces, and the guerrilla movement — and their role in the peace process. It presents a composite view from Salvadorans and others who experienced the war, and demonstrates both the importance of grounding humanitarian work in an understanding of the causes of conflict, and the limits on external intervention in determining the outcome.

Geoff Tansey et al.: *A World Divided*
London: Earthscan, 1994
Global militarism — the legacy of the Cold War — is, together with deepening economic polarisation between North and South, and environmental constraints on economic growth and development, seen as a central factor in contributing to insecurity. Using illustrations from both North and South to diagnose the problems caused by increasing militarism, the authors analyse the links between conflict, poverty, development, and environmental degradation; and ask why Northern governments pursue policies that exacerbate North-South tensions. They propose alternative policy measures for demilitarisation, sustainable development, and environmental management.

Martha Thompson: 'Empowerment and survival: humanitarian work in civil conflict', *Development in Practice*, 6/4 (November

1996) and 7/1 (February 1997) (forthcoming)
This two-part article explores the experience of living and working for an international NGO in a civil war whose roots lay in the inequitable distribution of power and wealth. Drawing on her 12 years' work in Central America, the author reflects on the demands and constraints placed on aid workers in a counter-insurgency war; and on how this shapes relationships with local organisations and NGOs. Empowerment and participation are examined from the perspective of people who refused to be war victims. In Part II, the author examines the impacts of war and political violence, both on those who survive and on local and inter-national workers who are concerned to address its causes and consequences.

UN Centre for Human Rights, *The Human Rights Fact Sheet series*
(available in English and in French), Geneva
These booklets deal with human rights issues that are under active consideration or of particular interest. The series (over 20 titles) offers a good account of basic human rights, what the UN is doing to promote and protect them, and the international machinery available to help realise those rights. Relevant titles include: *The International Bill of Human Rights*; *Advisory Services and Technical Assistance in the Field of Human Rights*; *Methods of Combating Torture*; *Enforced or Involuntary Disappearances*; *Summary or Arbitrary Executions*; *International Humanitarian Law and Human Rights*; *The Committee against Torture*; and *Human Rights and Refugees*.

UNESCO: *Non-military Aspects of International Security*
Paris: UNESCO, 1995
With the end of the Cold War, genuine security and stability cannot be ensured without addressing problems of a non-military character, in particular those related to environmental protection, economic and social development, the prevention of discrimination and violations of human rights, and extreme poverty and exclusion. The book considers new forms of international, regional, and

national security which would be compatible with aspirations for a world in which the ideals of democracy, human rights, and development can be realised.

UNHCR: *The State of the World's Refugees*
Annual report which examines the plight of displaced people and analyses the world's changing response to forced migration. Contains current statistics, together with appendices giving details of UNHCR's work, international instruments and their significance, and a bibliography. Recent reports have for example been entitled 'The Challenge for Protection' (1993), and 'In Search of Solutions' (1995).

UNRISD: *States of Disarray: The Social Effects of Globalisation*
Geneva: UNRISD (available in English, French, and Spanish), 1995
A comprehensive examination of contemporary problems that often underlie violent conflict and thus form a context for complex emergencies and post-war reconstruction. They include poverty, unemployment, inequality, and organised crime; as well as the declining responsibility of public institutions. Part I discusses the impact of globalisation on impoverishment, inequalities, work insecurity, weakening of institutions and social support systems, and the erosion of identities and values. Part II explores these developments in relation to crime, drugs, ethnic conflicts, and post-war reconstruction. Part III looks at the policy environment and the impact on various institutions of the principal forces shaping contemporary societies, stressing the links between insecurity, and social conflicts, including the rise of extremist movements.

UNRISD: *Ethnic Violence, Conflict Resolution and Cultural Pluralism*
Geneva, 1995
The report of a 1994 seminar on ethnicity and ethnic conflict. Since ethnicity tends to become most destructive when under threat, reducing tension depends on protecting people's rights to form ethnic loyalties, not on repressing

them. This does not imply support for policies to entrench ethnicity in social and political structures. Ethnicity evolves, and some ethnic markers lose significance, while new ones emerge.

Given the limitations of third-party intervention in ethnic conflicts, the report discusses policy approaches to facilitate accommodation in ethnically diverse societies. To promote peaceful relations, all groups need a shared interest in society as a whole. This sense of civic identity cannot be forced on people: it is one they must freely adopt. They are most likely to do so when their society respects and meets everyone's needs, including that of a sense of ethnic identity.

Thomas G Weiss and Larry Minear (eds)
Humanitarianism Across Borders: Sustaining Civilians in Times of War
Boulder and London: Lynne Rienner Publishers, 1993
This, the second of three books from the Humanitarianism and War Project (qv), is aimed both at humanitarian agencies and the concerned public. It comprises essays by nine authors who examine values, the use of military force, and the future shape of humanitarian institutions.

Aristide R Zolberg, Astri Suhrke and Sergio Aguayo: *Escape from Violence: Conflict and the Refugee Crisis in the Developing World*
Oxford and New York: Oxford University Press, 1989
This book provides both a theoretical framework for understanding the refugee phenomenon and a survey of refugee movements in Asia, Africa and Central America. Defining refugees as people with a 'well-founded fear of violence', it classifies them in three categories: activists, targets, and victims. The first two are generally able to claim refugee status, but the 'mere' victims are often denied international protection. The widespread violation of fundamental human rights by governments is the main cause of forced migration, and must be addressed as such by the international community.

Journals

DHA News (ISSN: 1020-2609)
Published five times a year by the UN Department of Humanitarian Affairs
Addresses issues concerning the provision of humanitarian assistance, particularly in conflict. For example, the May–June 1995 issue, 'Focus: Aid Under Fire', shows how distinctions between relief and development are increasingly blurred in practice, and NGO workers need negotiation and assessment skills as they face situations of violence and predation. As NGOs are often in the forefront of assisting in complex emergencies, they face a crisis of professionalism and the maintenance of integrity (credibility) in the growing humanitarian market.

Disasters: The Journal of Disaster Studies and Management (ISSN: 0361-3666)
Editors: Charlotte Benson and Joanna Macrae
Overseas Development Institute, UK
A journal for research on disasters, vulnerability, and relief and emergency management. The scope of the journal extends from disasters associated with natural hazards such as earthquakes and drought through to complex, conflict-related emergencies.

Gender and Development (ISSN: 1355-2074)
Published three times a year by Oxfam UK and Ireland
Editor: Caroline Sweetman
Each issue focuses on a specific theme in relation to gender and development initiatives, and is also published separately in book form. *Women and Emergencies* (1994) and *Women and Conflict* (1993) explore the experiences of women in situations of crisis, including civil and military strife.

Journal of Humanitarian Affairs (ISSN: 1360-0222)
Editors: Jim Whitman and Chris Alden
Electronic journal published at the University of Cambridge: http://www-jha.sps.cam.ac.uk/ (no print version available)
Brings together academics, policy-makers, and practitioners in the field of humanitarian assistance and aims to provide a means for policy debate, the sharing of lessons learned, and the fostering of cooperation within and between the different professions concerned with the many aspects of this work. Encompasses all aspects of humanitarian assistance, from early warning and emergency provision to post-conflict peace building and the transition to development.

Journal of Peace Research (ISSN: 0022-3433)
Published quarterly by Sage on behalf of the International Peace Research Institute, Oslo
Editors: Nils Peter Gleditsch and Malvern Lumsden
With a global focus on conflict and peace-making, the journal concentrates on the causes of violence, and on practical approaches to conflict-resolution.

Journal of Refugee Studies (ISSN: 0951-6328)
Published quarterly by Oxford University Press
Editor: Roger Zetter
A multidisciplinary journal dedicated to academic exploration of the problems of forced migration, and national and international responses to them. It promotes the theoretical development of refugee studies, new perspectives on refugee populations, and the reappraisal of current concepts, policies, and practice.

Research projects and relevant organisations

African Rights
Works on issues of human-rights abuses, conflict, famine, and civil reconstruction in Africa. Believes that the solutions to the problems of emergency humanitarian needs, political reconstruction, and accountability must be sought primarily among Africans; and that the role of international organisations should be chiefly to support Africans' own attempts to address these issues.

Hemispheric Migration Project (HMP)

Project Director: Mary Ann Larkin

Sponsored by the Centre for Immigration Policy and Refugee Assistance (CIPRA) at Georgetown University, the HMP supports research on refugees and labour migrants in the Americas. It encourages research on refugees and migration in the countries of origin, and publishes the findings for attention of policy-makers of sending and receiving countries. Publications include *From the Shadows to Center Stage: NGOs and Central American Refugee Assistance* (S. Aguayo, 1991); *Assistance and Control: Policies Toward Internally Displaced Populations in Guatemala* (AVANSCO 1990); *Refugee Policy Challenges: The Case of Nicaraguans in Costa Rica* (M. Ramirez, 1989); *Central Americans in Mexico City: Uprooted and Silenced* (L. O'Dogherty, 1989).

Humanitarianism and War: Learning the Lessons from Recent Armed Conflicts

Project Directors: Larry Minear and Thomas G Weiss

A major project assessing how international and multilateral agencies and NGOs might improve the response to the devastation resulting from war. Launched in 1991, it is sponsored by Brown University's Thomas J Watson Jr Institute for International Studies, and supported by many governments, UN organisations, and NGOs. Focusing on 'the interface between theory and practice', the project has published a prodigious range of material, from field manuals to high-level policy documents, from newspaper articles to scholarly papers.

Human Rights Watch (HRW)

Holding governments accountable if they violate the rights of their people, HRW conducts thorough investigations of human-rights abuses in some 70 countries, irrespective of political ideologies and alignments, or of ethnic and religious persuasions. HRW documents and denounces murders, disappearances, torture, arbitrary imprisonment, discrimination, and other abuses of internationally recognised human rights.

International Alert

An NGO engaged in research on the causes of violent conflict, training in mediation and negotiating skills, advocacy to persuade decision-makers to be devoted to conflict-resolution and prevention. International Alert also has regional and country programmes in East and West Africa, and South Asia.

International Committee of the Red Cross (ICRC)

ICRC's role is to protect and assist the victims of international and civil wars and conflicts. It is recognised as a neutral humanitarian agency in the Geneva Conventions and their Additional Protocols, which accord ICRC's delegates the authority to visit protected persons, such as prisoners of war, or civil internees. Its operations are conducted confidentially, and any human-rights abuses are raised privately with the controlling authorities. ICRC's unique mandate once made it one of the few international agencies working in armed conflict. However, the rapid growth of humanitarian NGOs, as well as the nature of contemporary warfare, are changing this. The ICRC takes a prime role in developing International Humanitarian Law, and has a wide range of publications, in English and in French.

Mennonite Central Committee

The relief service and development agency of the North American Mennonite and Brethren in Christ churches works in long-term development in over 50 countries, and considers peace education and peacemaking to be central to all aspects of its work. The MCC Peace Office, based in the USA, serves as a resource for MCC workers worldwide, and as a connection to the United Nations.

Minority Rights Group (MRG)

Publishes authoritative reports on minority groups all over the world, and on many issues relevant to emergency and crisis, for example: *Minorities and Human Rights Law*; *International Action against Genocide*; *The Social Psychology of Minorities*.

Quaker Peace and Service
General Secretary: Andrew C Clark
QPS, based in London, supports long-term programmes by sending experienced workers who contribute to reconciliation at all levels, sometimes working with the victims of wars or violence. QPS works with the UN in the areas of disarmament, human rights, refugees, and economic development through its staff in Geneva. It also works with decision makers, whether diplomats, politicians or funders, in non-official ways as intermediaries to encourage the peaceful resolution of conflict. In special circumstances QPS carries out non-official political reconciliation and communication work between opposing sides in war.

Refugee Policy Group (RPG)
An independent centre for policy research and analysis on refugee and related humanitarian issues, which publishes detailed reports and policy briefings and houses an extensive documentation centre, on matters concerning refugees and displaced persons. Of particular note is *Strengthening International Protection for Internally Displaced Persons* (1993).

Refugee Studies Programme
Programme Director: David Turton
The Refugee Studies Programme is part of the University of Oxford's International Development Centre. Established in 1982, RSP's aim is to increase understanding of the causes, consequences, and experiences of forced migration through multidisciplinary research, teaching, publications, seminars, and conferences. Independent of governments and assistance agencies, RSP provides a forum for discussion among refugees, researchers, practitioners, and policy makers.

Relief and Rehabilitation Network
Part of the Relief and Disasters Policy Programme of the Overseas Development Institute (ODI), which combines research, evaluation, and communications activities in collaboration with a range of bilateral, multilateral, NGO, and academic partners. The Network serves some 300 members in over 50 countries, mostly field-based. Mailings are in English and French, and members can obtain advice on technical and operational problems from within the ODI or via the Network itself.

Saferworld
An independent foreign affairs think-tank and public-education group, formed to alert governments to the need for new approaches to dealing with armed conflicts. Saferworld focuses on identifying key issues on which movement is possible, and drawing on the diverse contributions of a wide range of people, from political leaders to concerned members of the public, in order to generate creative solutions.

War-torn Societies Project, UNRISD and Programme for Strategic and International Security Studies (PSIS)
Project Director: Matthias Stiefel
Analyses experience of transforming a fragile cease-fire into a lasting political settlement that can provide the basis for sustainable development. Much research is conducted by in-country teams, coordinated via Geneva. The project seeks policy options for international donors, multilateral organisations, NGOs, and local authorities and organisations who are tackling these problems; and contributes to integrating international assistance — economic, humanitarian, political, and military — within a coherent policy framework. It produces various publications, including *After the Conflict: A review of selected sources on rebuilding war-torn societies* (1995), compiled by Patricia Weiss Fagen.

Addresses of publishers and other organisations listed

African Rights, 11 Marshalsea Road, London SE1 1EP, UK

CIIR (Catholic Institute for International Relations), Unit 3, Canonbury Yard, 109a New North Road, London N1 7BJ, UK

Centre for Immigration Policy and Refugee Assistance (CIPRA), Georgetown University, PO Box 2298-Hoya Station, Washington DC 20057-1001, USA

Collaborative for Development Action Inc, 26 Walker Street, Cambridge MA 02138, USA

Department of Humanitarian Affairs, Palais des Nations, 1211 Geneva, Switzerland

Earthscan Publications, 120 Pentonville Road, London N1 9JN, UK

Humanitarianism and War Project, Thomas J Watson Jr Institute for International Studies, Brown University, Box 1970, 2 Stimson Avenue, Providence, RI 02912, USA

Human Rights Watch, 485 Fifth Avenue, New York NY 10017-6014, USA

International Alert, 1 Glyn Street, London SE11 5HT, UK

International Council of Voluntary Agencies (ICVA), Case Postale 216, 1211 Geneva 21, Switzerland

International Committee of the Red Cross, 19 avenue de la Paix, 1202 Geneva, Switzerland

International Peace Research Institute, Fuglehauggata 11, 0260 Oslo, Norway

Latin America Bureau, 1 Amwell Street, London EC1R 1UL, UK

Mennonite Central Committee, 21 South 12th Street, PO Box 500, Akron PA 17501-0500, USA

Minority Rights Group, 379 Brixton Road, London SW9 7DE, UK

OECD, 2 rue André Pascal, 75775 Paris, Cedex 16, France

Overseas Development Institute, Regent's College, Inner Circle, Regent's Park, London NW1 4NS, UK

Oxfam Publishing, 274 Banbury Road, Oxford OX2 7DZ, UK

Oxford University Press, Walton Street, Oxford OX2 6DP, UK

Quaker Peace and Service, Friends House, Euston Road, London NW1 2BJ, UK

Refugee Policy Group, 1424 16th Street NW, Suite 401, Washington DC 20036, USA

Refugee Studies Programme, Queen Elizabeth House, 21 St Giles, Oxford OX1 3LA, UK

Lynne Rienner Publishers, 1800 30th St, Boulder, Colorado 80301, USA

St Martin's Press, 175 5th Avenue, New York NY 10010, USA

Saferworld, 33 Alfred Place, London WC1E 7DP, UK

Sage Publications, 6 Bonhill Street, London EC2A 4PU, UK

Save the Children Fund, 17 Grove Lane, London SE5 8RD, UK

The Fletcher School of Law and International Diplomacy, Program in International and US Refugee Policy, Tufts University, Medford, Massachussets 02155, USA

UN Centre for Human Rights, UN Office at Geneva, 8-14 avenue de la Paix, 1211 Geneva 10, Switzerland

UNESCO, 7 Place de Fontenoy, 75372 Paris 07 SP, France

UNHCR, Centre William Rappard, 154 rue de Lausanne, 1202 Geneva, Switzerland

UNRISD, Palais des Nations, 1211 Geneva, Switzerland

UN University Press, Toho Shimei Building, 15-1 Shibuya 2-chome, Shibuya-ku, Tokyo 150, Japan

United States Institute of Peace Press, 1550 M Street NW, Washington DC 20005, USA

Vietnam Veterans of America Foundation, 2001 S Street NW, Suite 740, Washington DC, USA

Washington Office on Latin America, 110 Maryland Avenue NE, Washington DC 20002, USA

Westview Press, 5500 Central Avenue, Boulder, Colorado 80301-2877, USA

The World Peace Foundation, 1 Eliot Square, Cambridge MA 02138-4952, USA

Zed Books, 9 Cynthia Street, London N1 9JF,

Development in Practice
a multi-disciplinary journal of development

Development in Practice is a forum for practitioners, policy makers, official aid agencies, NGOs, and academics to exchange information and analysis concerning the social dimensions of development and emergency relief work. As a multi-disciplinary journal of policy and practice, *Development in Practice* reflects a wide range of institutional and cultural backgrounds and a variety of professional experience. All articles are independently refereed. Each issue offers the following features:

- Editorial
- Main Articles
- Viewpoint
- Practical Notes
- Research Round-up
- Feedback
- Conference Reports
- Book Reviews
- Book Shelf
- News in Brief

The Editor welcomes contributions from any source, but actively encourages contributions from practitioners, and is pleased to hear from previously unpublished writers and authors whose first language is not English. Some editorial assistance may be offered where necessary. **Guidelines for Contributors** are available from the Editor, *Development in Practice*, c/o Oxfam, 274 Banbury Road, Oxford OX2 7DZ, UK.

'Here, in one single publication, are the latest tools, concepts and experiences, written in an accessible style, by and for development workers and managers. *Development in Practice* has proved itself a vital resource for professionals committed to learning and innovation.' — *Jethro Pettit, International Director, World Neighbors*

Development in Practice is published by Oxfam UK and Ireland. ISSN: 0961 4524

Electronic version

Development in Practice is also available in electronic form on the Internet via CatchWord Ltd, a worldwide electronic publishing services company. For further information about how to subscribe and to view *Development in Practice* via the CatchWord system, please connect to: http://www.catchword.co.uk

Subscriptions

Each volume (464 pages) is published in four issues (February, May, August, and November), with an index and translated abstracts at the end of the volume. *Development in Practice* provides subsidised subscriptions for individuals and organisations from countries listed in the current UN Human Development Report as 'developing countries'.

For further details of current subscription rates or to request a free inspection copy, please contact our distribution agent:

Carfax Publishing Company, PO Box 25, Abingdon, Oxfordshire, OX14 3UE, UK; fax: +44 (0)1235 401550; phone: +44 (0)1235 401000 (worldwide, 24 hours, 7 days a week); or Carfax Publishing Company, 875-81 Massachusetts Avenue, Cambridge, 02139 MA, USA; fax: + 1 617 354 6875; phone: 1-800 3541420; or Carfax Publishing Company, PO Box 352, Cammeray, NSW 2062, Australia; fax: +61 (0)29958 2376; phone +61 (0)2995 85329.

Development in Practice Readers

Series Editor: Deborah Eade

Each book in this new series offers a selection of articles from past issues of the journal *Development in Practice*, chosen to promote debate on a theme of current concern to the international development community. Each is introduced by a specially commissioned overview and ends with an annotated bibliography of current and classic titles.

Development and Social Diversity

introduced by Mary B. Anderson

The first book in the series considers how change affects different members of society in ways that reflect differences in their power and status, as defined by their age, gender, and cultural identity. By denying such diversity, development agencies risk excluding vulnerable social groups and actually increasing their poverty.
ISBN 0 85598 343 4   112 pages
1996

Oxfam Publications

Oxfam (UK and Ireland) publishes a wide range of books, manuals, journals, and resource materials for specialist, academic, and general readers. For a free catalogue, please write to Oxfam Publishing, 274 Banbury Road, Oxford OX2 7DZ, UK (telephone (0)1865 313922; e-mail publish@oxfam.org.uk).